DETERRENCE AND NUCLEAR PROLIFERATION IN THE TWENTY-FIRST CENTURY

DETERRENCE AND NUCLEAR PROLIFERATION IN THE TWENTY-FIRST CENTURY

Edited by Stephen J. Cimbala

PRAEGER

Westport, Connecticut
London

Library of Congress Cataloging-in-Publication Data

Deterrence and nuclear proliferation in the twenty-first century / edited by Stephen J. Cimbala.
    p.   cm.
  Includes bibliographical references and index.
  ISBN 0–275–96698–4 (alk. paper)
    1. Deterrence (Strategy).   2. Nuclear weapons.   3. Nuclear weapons—United States.   4.
  United States—Military policy.   5. World politics—21st century.   I. Cimbala, Stephen J.
  U162.6.D48   2001
  327.1'747—dc21   00–038526

British Library Cataloguing in Publication Data is available.

Library of Congress Catalog Card Number: 00–038526
ISBN: 0–275–96698–4

First published in 2001

Praeger Publishers, 88 Post Road West, Westport, CT 06881
An imprint of Greenwood Publishing Group, Inc.
www.praeger.com

Printed in the United States of America

The paper used in this book complies with the
Permanent Paper Standard issued by the National
Information Standards Organization (Z39.48–1984).

10 9 8 7 6 5 4 3 2 1

Contents

Introduction

Scholars, policy analysts, and government officials have engaged in a great debate since 1991 about the future of nuclear weapons in world politics. This debate has special significance for the United States at the end of the Cold War and the beginning of a new century. The United States was the first country to enter the nuclear age and the first to use nuclear weapons in war. Nuclear weapons helped to make the United States one of the world's two military superpowers throughout the Cold War. The United States relied on its nuclear weapons to deter a Soviet conventional attack on Western Europe, by including European allies within the umbrella of American nuclear protection (although this guarantee did not dissuade the French from going their own way on matters nuclear). Nuclear weapons made the United States, along with Britain, France, China, and the Soviet Union, a member of the club of five Cold War great powers.

The end of the Cold War and the demise of the Soviet Union have called into question all of the assumptions on which U.S. military strategy, and the role of nuclear weapons in that strategy, were based. Contributors to this volume offer diverse perspectives on the role of nuclear weapons in the new world order and on the implications of the new condition for U.S. security policy.

George H. Quester reviews the nuclear history through which we have lived, especially the evolution of U.S. Cold War nuclear strategy and policy. We can derive some insights about the future of nuclear weapons and arms control from a correct understanding of this nuclear history. Quester considers whether, and to what extent, the United States or other states actually benefited from the availability of nuclear weapons in the Cold War years. The asserted benefits of nuclear weapons in the hands of the Americans and their allies, or of those held by the Kremlin, were claims based on the abstract logic of deterrence. U.S. and Soviet nuclear weapons supposedly deterred each other. For the United States and NATO, nuclear weapons were thought to be the "equalizers" that deterred a Soviet attack on Western Europe despite NATO's apparent inferiority in conventional forces.

However, the U.S.–Soviet nuclear balance was not always one of approximate parity. A perceived imbalance could raise political tensions and exacerbate the management of crises. In the United States, critics of alleged U.S. nuclear inferiority at various times scored points in the domestic policy debate. The end of the Cold War and the Soviet collapse were attributed by some to the U.S. surge in arms expenditures during the 1980s that allegedly bankrupted the Soviet economy. Whether this was historical verity or conservative fable, the peaceful demise of the Soviet imperium left the United States as a singular global superpower. Whereas nuclear weapons served to compensate for Soviet conventional superiority in the Cold War years, the same weapons now became the preferred means by which the prospective opponents of the United States and NATO would seek to offset American superiority in high-technology conventional weapons, as displayed in the Gulf War of 1991.

The nuclear history covered by Quester placed deterrence at the center of U.S. security policy. Lewis A. Dunn argues that with the end of the Cold War, the collapse of the Soviet Union, and the emergence of hostile proliferators armed with weapons of mass destruction (including nuclear, biological, and chemical weapons), it is necessary and timely to rethink the role of deterrence in U.S. security policy. First, the logic of mutual deterrence in U.S.–Russian relations must be supplemented, if not supplanted, by a logic of strategic reassurance. Second, although deterrence will remain an important component of U.S. security policy, its modes of expression and implementation will need to be reoriented from Cold War fixations toward post–Cold War threats. Third, the United States must consider what role deterrrence can play, if any, in preventing subnational or terrorist groups from using weapons of mass destruction (WMD) against U.S. territory, forces, or allies.

Mutual strategic reassurance, according to Dunn, implies that increased nuclear transparency between the United States and Russia will become more important in the next decade than force reductions. Transparency includes opening up the decision-making processes and military activities in the two states. Some important accomplishments in U.S.–Russian nuclear transparency have already taken place, including U.S. assistance in the dismantling of some Russian nuclear force components and in the protection, control, and accounting for Russian nuclear weapons-grade materials. But more needs to be done, including the possible creation of a high-level U.S.–Russian Joint Working Group on 2010 Transparency Goals and Experiments.

Dunn acknowledges that a highly competent U.S. and allied deterrent posture will be part of a future tool kit to deal with new proliferation threats. But he notes that some of the principal assumptions and mechanisms of deterrence developed on the basis of Cold War experience must now be modified or abandoned. These formerly golden assumptions now undergoing intellectual meltdown include the following: that the United States can have high confidence in identifying the perpetrator of a WMD attack; that explicit reliance on the threat of nuclear punishment will influence planners of terrorist strikes by chemical, biological, or possibly even nuclear means; and that it is of first importance to avoid any direct clash between the military forces of U.S. or allied defenders and WMD attack perpetrators, in order to avoid undesired escalation to a wider war. This last assumption was dictated by the Cold War domination of every nuclear crisis by the overwhelming superiority of U.S. and Soviet strategic nuclear forces and by the fear that a clash between those states must be prevented at all costs. Now, however, deterrence may be reinforced by possible attackers' expectations that they will have an early and decisively unpleasant encounter with a U.S. or allied military response.

Given the evident transformations in geopolitics noted by Quester and Dunn, James Scouras argues for a new strategic calculus to inform U.S. policy makers and military planners. Scouras notes that Cold War methods of analysis and measures of effectiveness are of uncertain utility now. U.S. Cold War military assessments were dominated by models based on a two-sided arms race and deterrence problematique. Other scenarios were treated as variations on the main theme. The assumption was that whatever deterred a massive Soviet attack on Western Europe or on the United States would suffice to deter other challenges to U.S. and allied security. The conceptual pivot of this obsolete model, the U.S–Soviet global rivalry, has now vanished. A new strategic calculus must ask whether nuclear weapons are still relevant at all, and if so, under what conditions?

Scouras lays out the dimensions of a new strategic calculus by posing a series of pertinent questions and suggesting answers that are not necessarily reassuring to American policy makers. One pertinent question is whether nuclear deterrence is now really beside the point in the relationship between the United States and Russia. Although U.S.–Russian political relations are nonhostile, both states retain impressively large strategic nuclear arsenals into the next century. And

Russian politics, as Scouras notes, have been volatile and cannot be forecast with any accuracy, even by Russians. Another question, apart from Russia, is the spread of nuclear weapons and long-range delivery systems to "rogue" actors, including states with political agendas very much against the thrust of U.S. policy. U.S. policy toward Russia and toward rogue regimes may involve some unavoidable trade-offs. For example, a U.S. ballistic missile defense system designed to defeat light attacks from rogue regimes may be regarded by Russia as an effort to negate its deterrent and may therefore complicate implementation of U.S.–Russian START arms-reduction agreements.

Frederic S. Nyland examines some of the implications of deep reductions in the U.S. and Russian strategic nuclear arsenals. He has two objectives in doing so. First, Nyland wants to develop hypotheses about the relationship between first-strike stability and various levels of nuclear force reduction. Second, he considers the relationship between the proportions of strategic nuclear weapons on alert and political stability. First-strike stability, defined as the disincentive for either side to strike first, is influenced by two sets of variables in Nyland's analysis: force posture and the deployment of antiballistic missile defenses by both sides. Nyland considered the implications of missile defenses under the assumption of offensive force reductions to 2,500 and 800 offensive warheads on each side.

In his analysis, Nyland found that the impact of antimissile defenses was destabilizing: At each level of offenses, deployment of additional defensive interceptors steadily decreased first-strike stability. This effect is the result of the ability of a first striker to use defenses to negate the retaliatory strike of the other side, permitting attacks with impunity. However, countermeasures by the retaliator, such as decoys, mitigate the effect of defenses. In addition, Nyland acknowledges that small numbers of ballistic missile defense (BMD) deployments (say, 100 interceptors or fewer), would permit protection against rogue state attacks without a major, deleterious effect on the measure of first-strike stability. Beyond first-strike stability, Nyland also measures one aspect of the more inclusive and elusive problem of geopolitical stability: politicomilitary tensions as manifest in the alert or nonalert status of strategic nuclear forces. He concludes that first-strike stability and geopolitical stability can be preserved at acceptable levels even if U.S. and Russian warheads are reduced below START II levels.

William C. Martel argues that U.S. nonproliferation policy may have worked during the Cold War, but its time has past: Its failure in the post–Cold War world is almost foreordained. U.S. blanket opposition to all cases of nuclear proliferation beyond the nuclear signatories to the Nonproliferation Treaty (NPT) (the United States, the Soviet Union, Britain, France, and China) prevailed during the Cold War and, in that context, it was reasonably successful. But the same policy and its use by international regimes to enforce a ban on the further spread of nuclear weapons and delivery systems is no longer credible. According to Martel, a new U.S. stance on nonproliferation is needed that can distinguish permissible cases of proliferation from impermissible ones. Permissible cases of proliferation are those in which states agree to live within acceptable norms and standards of international behavior.

Additional states beyond those currently in possession of nuclear weapons will see nuclears as part of the solution to their security dilemmas. International institutions and regimes designed to keep the cork in the bottle of nuclear weapons' spread cannot prevent determined state actors from going nuclear, as the cases of India and Pakistan in 1998 and the near misses of North Korea and Iraq illustrate (the former pursued a weapons-development program while a signatory to the Nonproliferation Treaty, and the latter was developing a nuclear arsenal while under inspection by the International Atomic Energy Agency).

In the twenty-first century too many states will possess the technical know-how and the resources to develop and deploy nuclear weapons for Cold War nonproliferation strategies to be effective. In addition to calling for a differentiated U.S. nonproliferation strategy that makes a distinction between stabilizing and destabilizing cases of proliferation, Martel also recommends that U.S. leaders not contribute to the prevalent perception that nuclear weapons are the only ticket to major-power status. One of the ironic consequences of pandemic U.S. public diplomacy against nuclear weapons, according to Martel, has been to emphasize to potential U.S. adversaries how potentially important and useful nuclear weapons really are for various purposes, including the dissuasion of U.S. foreign military interventions.

Stephen J. Cimbala considers whether, in view of a transformed international environment and nonhostile political relations between the United States and Russia, the United States will have the option to reduce its Cold War reliance on a "triad" of strategic nuclear forces. He first establishes the continuing relevancy of nuclear weapons in the new world order and of a modified deterrent relationship between the United States and Russia. Cimbala then considers the need for a U.S. triad and possible options of the triad within the context of two force levels: START III reductions to 2,000–2,500 warheads on each side, or lower than START III levels of 1,500 per side.

He concludes that from an arms-control perspective that emphasizes the fulfillment of the requirements of minimum deterrence based on assured retaliation, the United States could operate at START III or lower levels with a dyad instead of a triad of strategic nuclear forces. A U.S. strategic nuclear dyad would rely on submarine-launched missiles and bombers, doing without intercontinental land-based ballistic missiles. Mathematically, the United States could also fulfill the requirements of assured retaliation by basing its deterrent on a single force only: the fleet ballistic missile submarine force (SSBNs). On the other hand, basing the entire retaliatory force at sea is politically contentious (on account of the elimination of service roles and missions) and dubious, according to some expert opinion, from the standpoint of military strategy. According to this opinion, the Cold War strategic nuclear triad had a synergistic or transactional survivability because each leg of the force posed different problems for a putative attacker.

1

Relating Nuclear Weapons to American Power

George H. Quester

Most analysts of military and foreign affairs would agree that nuclear weapons have been important to the U.S. world position since 1945.[1] Only a few would argue that such weapons have made no difference, that history would have evolved more or less the same even if Einstein had been wrong and atomic bombs had never been developed.[2]

The intention of this chapter will be to sort the periods of time since the end of World War II when such weapons have made greater or lesser contributions to American world power, and then to project the influence of nuclear weapons into the future. Among the important factors here will be whether and when other powers acquire nuclear weapons, what the confrontation of traditional ("conventional") military forces has been, and whether the political background has produced basic conflicts between the United States and such other powers.

Analysts of broader international relations have sometimes focussed on whether the world is "bipolar" or "multipolar" amid contending theories of which structure and distribution of power is the more likely to produce peace.[3] The end of the Cold War has even produced speculation about a "unipolar" world, where the United States is presumably far ahead of all the other states in the military or other power it can bring to bear in potential conflicts.[4]

While this array of alternative interpretations of the distribution of power in the world is not based only on nuclear weapons, it has often been tied fairly closely to such weapons of mass destruction. Among the questions we will be sorting here are whether and when the United

States has benefitted from the existence of nuclear weapons, and when Americans would instead be inclined to wish that such weapons had not been introduced. Also to be examined, since power is typically a relative consideration, is whether and when other countries have benefitted from the possession, or even rumored possession, of nuclear weapons, and how this would relate to "American power."

Looking to the future, the prospect is now much discussed in the United States (not always with the greatest seriousness, however) of a total elimination of nuclear weapons, a move to a "nuclear-free world."[5] The analysis and research that would be required to do justice to this last possibility will exceed the space available here, but it will also relate to the continuing theme of American nuclear power.

THE RELEVANT PERIODS OF TIME

The periods of time that are significantly different might be broken apart as follows:

- 1945 to 1949, when only the United States possessed nuclear weapons and could presumably use such weapons without having to fear anyone else's nuclear retaliation.

- 1949 to approximately 1956, when the Soviet Union was known to possess such weapons but the American arsenal was seen to be substantially larger (i.e., a period of American superiority rather than monopoly). This was a period when the delivery systems for carrying such nuclear weapons to targets would have been bomber aircraft, a delivery system that suggested a low degree of crisis stability, since striking first would have great advantages over letting the other side strike first.[6]

- 1957 to 1961, when fears of a "missile gap" (this had been preceded by earlier fears of a "bomber gap") had conjured up possibilities of the Soviet Union launching a nuclear war in which it could escape American retaliation.[7]

- 1961 to the late 1960s, when the Soviet missile gap had been proved illusory and a United States superiority was once again generally recognized. As missiles based in concrete silos underground—or, more important, on board submarines wandering the oceans—were to be deployed in both the United States and the Soviet Union, this was now presumably a period of much higher crisis stability, as striking first might use up many more of one's own missiles than could be destroyed on the other side.[8]

- The later 1960s to the mid-1970s, when the world came to speak of a general nuclear parity, where the U.S. and the Soviet nuclear arsenals came to seem very comparable.

- The mid-1970s to the early 1980s, when analysts began speaking, in various measures, of an emerging Soviet nuclear superiority and of the risk of a "window of vulnerability."[9] This was a period in which crisis stability was to come somewhat into doubt again, because intercontinental missiles were expected to become much more accurate on each side, allowing for very direct attacks on opposing missile silos, and because both sides had deployed multiple-warhead missiles (MIRVs), such that there would again be a greater incentive to strike first if war was likely.

- The early 1980s until 1989, when Reagan's expenditures on nuclear weapons systems and on the Strategic Defense Initiative (SDI) seemed once again to be turning this Soviet advantage around, so that the U.S. nuclear force, whatever this term might now mean, would again be superior.[10]

- 1989 to the present, when the political collapse of communism, first in the Warsaw Pact and then in the Soviet Union itself, drastically altered the political base for the nuclear confrontation, and when substantial reductions in the totals of nuclear weapons were agreed upon.[11]

What also needs to be factored into this discussion of American nuclear power is the proliferation of such nuclear weapons to other nations, as Britain detonated its own first atomic bomb in 1952, France did so in 1960, and Communist China in 1964. The Indian detonation of a "peaceful nuclear explosive" followed a decade later in 1974, amid rumors since the 1960s that Israel was working toward acquiring such weapons, and similar rumors about Pakistan, South Africa, and a string of other possible "nth" nuclear-weapons states.[12] In the spring of 1998 India detonated five more nuclear devices, and Pakistan openly tested nuclear explosives in response.

THE BACKGROUND OF THE
CONVENTIONAL CONFRONTATION

The dramatic changes of 1989, symbolized most by the tearing down of the Berlin Wall, might be seen by some as now making issues of American power versus Russian power basically irrelevant as the political tensions of democratic versus Marxist ideology were removed. To the extent that considerations of power might still remain important, however, even between two democracies, 1989 is very important in a different way, because it realigned the great bulk of conventional military power, the traditional confrontation of tanks and ground forces, in the opposite direction from what had applied through the nuclear age.

From 1945 to 1989, through all the periods broken out separately in our list, the premise was always that Moscow commanded the geopolitical advantage in the central position it occupied in Eurasia, and that it held the advantage in the force totals it could deploy from this central position, the "Asian hordes" and innumerable armored divisions it could despatch.

After 1989, and after the breakup of the Soviet Union itself in 1991, the United States now actually exceeded the Russian Federation in total population. With the Warsaw Pact disbanded and the Central European former members of the Pact petitioning to join NATO, the confrontation of conventional forces thus presumably favored the United States for the first time since Hitler had been defeated, as Russia might now have to fear "American hordes" in the size and fighting power of the U.S. conventional forces.

This change in the conventional military background, against which any additional influence of nuclear forces has to be projected, may in the end be as important as any of the changes in the nuclear situation we have outlined.[13]

THE YEARS OF THE AMERICAN NUCLEAR MONOPOLY

It might be easiest to evaluate the impact of nuclear weapons on American power for the years before the first detected Soviet nuclear detonation in 1949. The American monopoly on nuclear weapons allowed the United States to end the war with Japan perhaps two years earlier than most people had expected. And the same monopoly was widely seen, as Winston Churchill noted in a famous speech of 1948, as having deterred Soviet armored forces from advancing across Western Europe.[14]

If the Soviet Union had attacked (i.e., had exploited the geopolitical advantages it held at the center of the Eurasian continent and the enormous advantage in ground forces it maintained after 1945, when Western conventional disarmament was much more extensive and rapid than that of Stalin's armies), there seemed to be little doubt that the United States would have used its nuclear weapons in retaliation, just as it had punished Japan at Hiroshima and Nagasaki for the Pearl Harbor attack.

Puzzles remain about this period, one of them pertaining to the belated disclosures that the United States did not produce nuclear weapons in serious numbers in 1946 or 1947, such that its nuclear deterrent was somewhat of a bluff.[15] A broader puzzle is why Americans gave so little consideration to preventive war in these years, to a policy of imposing rather than merely proposing the Baruch Plan, or imposing any other arrangement to keep the Soviet Union from getting atomic bombs of its own.[16]

Some analysts would explain the American failure to exploit the monopoly more (i.e., to exploit it so as to maintain it) by the shortage of actual U.S. nuclear weapons produced, but this merely pushes the puzzle deeper, for it should not have been impossible for the Truman administration to keep some bomb production teams at work. After the tensions that emerged with the USSR in 1947, and especially after the 1948 Berlin blockade, the production rate of American nuclear weapons was indeed stepped up.

Most Americans, if asked to reflect on why their country did not exploit the nuclear monopoly to force disarmament and democratization on the USSR (before 1949, when the first and most serious instance of nuclear proliferation was to occur), would cite the fundamental morality of American democracy, which could not bring itself to initiate a war. American nuclear weapons would have come into use, and Moscow and other Soviet cities would have been destroyed, and democracy would have been brought to Russia some four decades earlier, if Stalin had ever initiated an outright war of aggression in these years, just as Japan had suffered nuclear attack and then democratization as the consequence of having initiated World War II. But Stalin wisely did not yet launch such aggression.

THE YEARS OF "AMERICAN SUPERIORITY": 1949–1957

Once the Soviet Union had even a few atomic bombs, many strategic analysts would have concluded that everything was changed, that American nuclear power would now be neutralized by the prospect that American cities would also be destroyed if Soviet cities were destroyed.[17]

The result, by the analysis of a long series of "limited war" arguments that emerged in the 1950s, was that nuclear weapons would be held back from use in warfare by a process of mutual deterrence, even while other weapons would come into use. Stalin's sanctioning of Kim Il-Sung's blatant aggression against South Korea in June of 1950 seemingly supplied the model.

There were some American strategic analysts within the U.S. Air Force and elsewhere who saw continuing advantage in the fact that the United States had larger numbers of nuclear weapons and had a better ability to deliver them. Proposals for a preventive war exploiting this advantage were given a hearing of sorts in the broad strategic analysis conducted in the first months of the Eisenhower administration in 1953, but were quickly dismissed.[18] The simple fact that the Soviets might be able to deliver atomic bombs to destroy one or two American cities, and even more assuredly could destroy a number of West European cities, cities with which Americans very much identified, was regarded as sufficient to deter an American initiation of nuclear warfare.

Some analysts of limited war thus saw Western Europe to be as wide open to a Soviet armored attack as South Korea, as the United States would have to avoid any use of nuclear weapons if Moscow only utilized conventional weapons in an armored advance, because the untouched American cities would be a hostage against any nuclear escalation. In future years Pierre Gallois would develop this into an argument for a French acquisition of a separate nuclear force.[19] If Soviet tanks were rolling toward Paris, Gallois and others argued, an American president would be unwilling to initiate the use of nuclear weapons because he still had too much to lose. But the French nuclear force would come into use in a reprisal on Moscow, because France at this stage would have nothing left to lose.

Yet the credibility of the American "nuclear umbrella," of what was often referred to as "extended nuclear deterrence," was hardly to be written off so definitely here, and the debate about whether American nuclear weapons might effectively shield the NATO countries against a Soviet (Warsaw Pact) conventional attack indeed continued until the very end of the Cold War.[20]

There were several ways in which the American threat to use nuclear weapons might still be made credible, even if New York would be destroyed in the process. If the Moscow leadership saw that the United States had committed itself, it would never launch the European aggression in the first place, and nuclear devastation would never have to befall the United States or anyplace else.

First, the United States was committed to the formal treaty obligations of the NATO treaty. Americans are legalistic people who take treaties seriously. Second, American troops were stationed in substantial numbers in West Germany and elsewhere in Europe. Their official role was now, after 1949, to try to maintain a conventional defense of Western Europe, which might have been seen as a sign of the American reluctance to initiate nuclear warfare. But if their effort to hold back a Soviet tank onslaught was unsuccessful (which was very likely), their being killed or taken prisoner would enrage the American public and government, possibly almost as much as a direct nuclear attack on North America.

Third, American tactical nuclear weapons were now deployed in West Germany. Officially, these, like the American ground forces assigned to NATO, were intended to help blunt a Soviet armored advance. Yet such weapons were very likely to come into use even if they were not effective in stopping Soviet armored columns, to come into use (despite the analysis of American limited war theorists,[21] or of Gallois) merely because of where they were located, in the direct path of the Soviet advance.

For the entire length of the Cold War debates ranged about the reliability of such mechanisms in maintaining the credibility of American extended deterrence. For the same duration of the Cold War the premise remained that the Warsaw pact probably retained the military advantage if a war were to be fought only with conventional forces because of the greater numbers of tanks that Moscow had acquired and the geographic position that the Soviet advance of 1945 had achieved.

Under such circumstances, the net impact of the existence of nuclear weapons, however uncertain and debated this impact might be, was thought to be a "great equalizer," a reinforcement for NATO and the free world against the Soviet Union and the satellites it dominated.

Some analyses concluded that this American gain from the existence of nuclear weapons, the possible credibility of extended nuclear deterrence, depended on American superiority in this kind of weapon. Others argued that once the American monopoly on such weapons was gone it made little difference whether one side or the other was superior in such weapons. Under all circumstances it would be suicidal for the United States to go through with its threats to use such weapons in response to a Soviet tank attack on Europe or South Korea because the resulting escalation would lead to a global nuclear holocaust in which American cities were destroyed. But it would also be very dangerous for the USSR to test this American willingness to commit suicide on behalf of its allies, and the result would be that the Kremlin would be deterred from exploiting its tanks, its general advantage in conventional war.

BOMBER GAPS AND MISSILE GAPS: SOVIET SUPERIORITY?

In the late 1950s concerns arose that the United States might no longer be superior in nuclear forces (whatever this concept might mean), but might actually fall behind the Soviets. The very worst fear was that the Soviets would somehow acquire an ability to catch all the American nuclear forces on the ground and escape retaliation, thus achieving for Moscow the same monopoly of weapons of mass destruction that America had held between 1945 and 1949, with presumably disastrous consequences for freedom in the world.

One version of such a threat emerged with rumors of a "bomber gap," as the USSR might secretly be acquiring large numbers of jet bombers and the United States might not have dispersed its own bomber force widely and securely enough to survive a Soviet first-strike attack. This danger proved illusory, as the U.S. Air Force Strategic Air Command (SAC) indeed dispersed its forces, in part in response to a worrisome study of bomber vulnerability conducted by the RAND Corporation.[22]

A second even more frightening version of this threat of Soviet monopoly emerged with the race to develop intercontinental ballistic missiles, a race the USSR seemed to be winning, dramatically illustrated with the Soviet launching of the Sputnik satellite in 1957. If the

USSR possessed missiles and the United States only possessed bombers, it might again be possible for Moscow to launch a first-strike nuclear attack which, in less than thirty minutes, caught all the American nuclear forces on the ground, allowing Khrushchev to dictate peace terms to the world much as the United States had exploited its nuclear monopoly of 1945 to dictate peace terms to Japan.[23]

The missile gap also proved illusory, as the United States expedited work on its own missiles and Soviet production of intercontinental missiles had run into problems despite Khrushchev's boast that they were coming off the assembly line "like sausages." President Eisenhower was given valuable reassuring information about the absence of a missile gap by his secret U-2 reconnaissance flights over Siberia. Without such flights, American fears would have been greater, and the ultimate production of American missiles would have risen in response to such fears.[24]

The years from 1957 to 1961 nonetheless illustrate a time when the world saw nuclear weapons as perhaps gravely endangering American power, and endangering the very survival of the free world.

A STABLE PARITY: 1961–1970

The confrontation of bomber force against bomber force, or of the first generation of land-based missiles, had thus set up possibilities of a nuclear first strike that would give the aggressor another monopoly of nuclear power. The fears of 1957 to 1961 were that Moscow might be able to launch such an attack.

At all points between 1949 and 1965 there were also some prospects that the United States might be able to launch such an attack. Because the Americans had not exploited their total nuclear monopoly before 1949, most people would have seen the United States as much less threatening, and much less likely to initiate a war. Yet the interlocking logic of crisis instability suggested that each of the nuclear powers would have sensed in the 1960s that it was better off being the first to strike rather than the second. If radar screens or other intelligence sources suggested that the opposing power was about to launch a nuclear attack, it would have been militarily preferable to preempt that attack, and the result might well have been a World War III that neither side wanted.[25]

The development of nuclear missiles was accompanied by technological breakthroughs after 1960 in the deployment of such missiles on board a submarine wandering around the high seas, a submarine that would be invulnerable to the first strike of any missiles or bombers from the other side because its very location would be invisible and unknown. As the United States deployed its first Polaris missile-carrying submarine in 1960, and as the USSR eliminated problems in its own submarine-based missile force by the mid-1960s, the nuclear confrontation thus entered a much more stable phase, where neither side might be in such a hurry to fire in a crisis, but would rather see advantages in waiting. Since Moscow or Washington could retaliate on second strike days or weeks later from submarine-based forces imposing a devastating thermonuclear retaliation on the opposing side, there would be no need for haste.

In the sense that American nuclear power should reduce the chances of war, the 1960s thus ushered in a period where the chances of a World War III were markedly reduced. The question remained, as already outlined, of whether nuclear weapons would also work to reduce the chances of a conventional war and deter Moscow from despatching the Warsaw Pact armored forces westward into Europe.

As noted, some would have seen the American escalatory threats of flexible response as depending on American superiority. Others would even have seen such escalation as more credible when the crisis stability between the two superpowers was less; that is, would have seen American nuclear deterrence on behalf of NATO as more plausible when bomber forces faced each other, rather than when submarine-based missile forces were in place.

But those who believed in the continuing American nuclear umbrella for the democracies of Europe would have relied instead on the other links of commitment noted: the treaties and pledges of American honor and the forward presence of American troops and American "theater" nuclear weapons.

THE WINDOW OF VULNERABILITY

One enters another round of the role of nuclear power in the Cold War by the middle of the 1970s, when the total number of nuclear weapons procured by the Soviet Union surged well ahead of the total at which the United States had levelled off, and when some of the stabilizing impact of missiles was again to come into question.

Submarine-based missiles would continue to be basically invulnerable, but land-based intercontinental missiles were to become a much more attractive target again for counterforce first-strike attacks. Missiles were now becoming much more accurate, so that they could land virtually on top of any missile silo they were attacking, and missiles had been fitted with multiple warheads on each side, so that the contents of one missile silo, if fired first, could destroy a number of missile silos on the other side.

This combination of enhanced accuracy and the "MIRVing" of land-based missiles with multiple warheads moved the confrontation back in the unstable direction of the 1950s, when whoever struck first would be better off militarily in terms of missiles left after the exchange compared to whoever had waited to strike.[26]

The decrease in crisis stability would have to have been seen as lessening the nuclear contribution to American security as the chances of an unwanted war would be increased again. Worsening the American power position even more, according to the pessimistic analysis presented by the Committee on the Present Danger in the late 1970s (an organization playing an important part in the 1980 election of President Ronald Reagan), was the substantial growth in the size of the Soviet nuclear arsenal.

The worrisome picture was now painted of a "window of vulnerability," a time in the early 1980s where the USSR could enforce its will on the United States by launching a missile attack on all the land-based missiles and bomber bases of the United States, eliminating such forces entirely while retaining a substantial portion of the Soviet forces as a bargaining tool for the negotiations to come.[27]

What made this scenario somewhat less worrisome, however, was the fact that the submarine-based missiles of the U.S. Navy would still be in place after such an attack, able to inflict horrible retaliation on the USSR. The worst image one could forecast for Soviet nuclear predominance in the 1980s thus could not match the fearsome forecasts of those who had foreseen a missile gap in the early 1960s.

Yet the image was nonetheless one of an end to American superiority in strategic nuclear weapons, replaced by a parity, or worse, by a Soviet superiority in the nuclear realm.

The Reagan election campaign argued that this needed to be headed off with an increase in defense spending. Reagan's victory over Jimmy Carter in 1980 has to be traced to a number of factors, both domestic and international, but the concern of American voters about a decline in American nuclear power played a role.

SDI: AMERICAN "SUPERIORITY" AGAIN

The window of vulnerability may always have been unreal, for the reasons cited, because the United States retained a tremendous retaliatory capability in its submarine-based force. If anyone's submarines were at all plausibly vulnerable to an opposing counterforce attack, it would have been those of the Soviet Navy, which were much noisier, and American antisubmarine warfare (ASW) techniques were much more advanced.[28]

The Reagan administration nonetheless announced steps to increase the readiness of all American armed forces, nuclear as well as conventional, in a substantial enhancement of defense spending, a portion of which had already been started at the end of the Carter administration. Responding to moral criticisms that mutual-assured destruction depended on the targeting of innocent civilians as the means to preserve peace, Reagan announced in 1983 that he was committed to a Strategic Defense Initiative, which would develop new technologies to shield American cities against incoming missile attacks.

While skeptics about the feasibility of a perfect antimissile defense derided the SDI, this program amounted to another extensive enhancement of the general research funding for U.S. nuclear and other weapons systems, and it apparently convinced Moscow that the United States might surge ahead in various layers of the strategic confrontation.[29] The Soviet leadership responded by renewed military investments on its side to outrace the United States in the tools of nuclear military power, and this is widely seen as having broken the back of the generally inefficient and overstrained Soviet economy, leading to the collapse of the Warsaw Pact, and then of the Soviet Union itself; that is, to the Western victory ending the Cold War.

AFTER THE COLD WAR

All through the Cold War, as noted, there was a serious debate about whether American nuclear power could contribute to the security of the NATO countries and South Korea, and whether this contribution was at all related to the general background factor of American or Soviet nuclear superiority. The end of the Cold War made this issue largely moot, as the Warsaw Pact ceased to exist, Germany was unified, and Soviet forces were pulled back far to the East, with Russia now actually being outnumbered by America in simple manpower.

Supporters of Ronald Reagan's policies would argue that American nuclear strength, and Reagan's application of American resources and technology to reinforcing that strength, had played an important role in achieving this ultimate NATO security, winning the Cold War.[30] The Soviets had, for whatever reason, initiated a race to try to dominate the world with a vast nuclear arsenal. The Americans had responded to the challenge, had proven to be more able to run the race, and the USSR economy had collapsed in the effort.

With the race thus having been won, and with democratic political practices coming to Russia under President Yeltsin, it was possible for Reagan's successor, President George Bush, to negotiate a substantial reduction in nuclear forces with Yeltsin, beginning the reductions with the most destabilizing of such forces, the land-based multiple-warhead missiles.[31]

Returning to the issue of extended nuclear deterrence (the threat of nuclear escalation as a deterrent to the opposing side's launching a conventional aggression), much of the logic of advantages here would now be reversed.

Until 1989 a purely conventional-war situation would have favored Moscow and disadvantaged the United States and its allies; hence, there was reason for Americans to be glad that nuclear weapons had been invented. After 1989 Americans had very little need for a nuclear "equalizer," because, as demonstrated in the Desert Storm operation liberating Kuwait from Iraqi occupation, the conventional advantage now lay with the United States and its allies. Hence there was now reason for Americans to regret that nuclear weapons had been invented, and to be increasingly concerned about their proliferation to possibly irresponsible states around the world.[32] Conversely, any states allegedly now fearing American hegemony might have shifted to welcoming the existence of nuclear weapons as an equalizer of sorts.

The Soviet Union, all through the Cold War, had tried to induce the European countries to agree to a "nuclear free zone" and/or to policies of "no first use" of nuclear weapons to eliminate the prospect of nuclear escalation. Wary cynics saw this as Moscow's effort to free Europe for Soviet conventional aggression, and had responded with a continuing of NATO's blurry flexible response strategy, which always kept open the prospect of nuclear escalation where conventional defenses could not suffice.

Illustrating how the polarity of such strategic logic has been reversed, the Russian military showed an interest under Yeltsin in a flexible response doctrine for the future, moving away from any commitments to no first use.[33]

Now that the former members of the Warsaw Pact are petitioning to become members of NATO and the conventional armed forces of the United States, even without its allies, seem so much to outclass those of Russia, it might be Moscow's turn to welcome the existence of nuclear weapons, and to play with escalation threats as the counter to conventional power, with the United States conversely now having reason to wish that nuclear weapons could be eliminated.

THE GENERAL IMPACT OF NUCLEAR
PROLIFERATION ON POWER

As noted, Pierre Gallois presented a very open and rational case that French nuclear weapons were needed, because the United States would not escalate to a nuclear war if France or another European state were being subjected to only a conventional attack.

The first round of nuclear proliferation had come in 1949, when the Soviet Union had acquired nuclear weapons, in a great variety of ways thus challenging the American power that had been derived from a monopoly of nuclear weapons. The next instance of such proliferation came with the British nuclear detonation of 1952. The British independent nuclear force was never really explained in so clear a logic as the French, which came along in 1960, but was always more broadly justified as a reinforcement for Britain's role in the world, and British power and importance.

China was the last country to openly acknowledge acquiring nuclear weapons, with its detonation in 1964. India test detonated a "peaceful nuclear explosive" in 1974. There was substantial reason to believe that Israel and Pakistan had acquired numbers of nuclear weapons as "bombs in the basement," without openly admitting to their existence or having to detonate them.[34] Then, 1998 saw India and Pakistan exchanging rounds of nuclear test detonations. The array of motives for such proliferation vary from pursuit of national importance to the basic reinsurance of national independence against the possible conventional military of other states.

We are dealing here mainly with American power as it has been reinforced or undermined by nuclear weapons, so the discussion will concentrate on the American opposition to nuclear proliferation, which became clear since 1964 in backing the NPT presented to the world in 1968, and in other components of what is sometimes labelled the "nonproliferation regime."

Hard-headed realist analysts of international politics would see the American opposition to nuclear proliferation as intended simply to enhance and retain American power, as the "haves" will always try to impose restraint on the "have-nots." This has been the picture often put forward by diplomats and strategic analysts in India and China, and at times in the past in France.

Yet a more nuanced analysis would see American opposition to the spread of nuclear weapons as reflecting other concerns, substantially removed from power. The proliferation of such weapons may, under some circumstances, increase the likelihood of war. And such proliferation may very much increase the destructiveness if wars were to occur, between India and Pakistan, between Israel and the Arab states, between North and South Korea, and so forth.[35]

American advocates of arms control, supporting both nonproliferation and the elimination of existing nuclear arsenals, sometimes go so far as to argue that nuclear weapons are not relevant to national power and standing, that people will not defer any more to a state with atomic bombs than to a state without. Yet such a high-minded attitude surely goes too far. The United States defers much more to North Korea, which is suspect of seeking nuclear weapons, than to Fidel Castro's regime in

Cuba, which is not. The very urgency that Americans and others assign to nonproliferation generates an importance, and thus some additional power, for the countries that are capable of such proliferation.

Communist China is more powerful because it has atomic bombs than it would have been without, and so are France and Britain, and so is Russia, and so are Israel and Pakistan. The American opposition to such additional nuclear-weapons possession (indeed, it is hardly clear that the United States was fully opposed to France, Britain, or Israel converging on nuclear arsenals) is indeed derived from considerations other than power. But American power would be greater if there were fewer other nuclear weapons arsenals in the world.

NOTES

1. See Robert Jervis, *The Meaning of the Nuclear Revolution* (Ithaca, N.Y.: Cornell University Press, 1989).

2. For one very interesting illustration, John E. Mueller, *Retreat from Doomsday: The Obsolescence of Major War* (New York: Basic Books, 1989).

3. An important example is Kenneth Waltz, "The Stability of a Bipolar World," *Daedalus* 23 (1964): 881–909.

4. See Charles Krauthammer, "The Unipolar Moment," *Foreign Affairs* 70, no. 1 (1990–1991): 23–33.

5. For examples of such a vision, see Michael Mazarr and Alexander Lennon, eds., *Toward a Nuclear Peace* (New York: MacMillan, 1994).

6. A major illustration of such concerns is to be found in Albert Wohlstetter, "The Delicate Balance of Terror," *Foreign Affairs* 37 (1959): 211–234.

7. For an example of such concerns, see James Gavin, *War and Peace in the Space Age* (New York: Harper, 1958).

8. An analysis predicting the advantages of such submarine basing of missiles is to be found in Oskar Morgenstern, *The Question of National Defense* (New York: Random House, 1959).

9. See Michael Nacht, *The Age of Vulnerability* (Washington, D.C.: Brookings Institution, 1985).

10. An analysis suggesting a recovery of a meaningful American nuclear superiority can be found in Alexei Arbatov, "START II, Red Ink, and Boris Yeltsin," *Bulletin of the Atomic Scientists* 49, no. 4 (1993): 16–21.

11. For an overview of post–1989 nuclear developments, see Michele Flourney, ed., *Nuclear Weapons After the Cold War* (New York: HarperCollins, 1993).

12. A useful survey of the nuclear proliferation problem can be found in Lewis A. Dunn, *Controlling the Bomb* (New Haven: Yale University Press, 1982).

13. On the emerging U.S. superiority in conventional weapons, see William J. Perry, "Desert Storm and Deterrence," *Foreign Affairs* 70 (1991): 66–82.

14. Speech of March 25, 1949, reprinted in *Winston Churchill: His Complete Speeches* (New York: Bowker, 1974), vol. VII, pp. 7795–7781.

15. On the numbers of American nuclear weapons in these years, see David A. Rosenberg, "U.S. Nuclear Stockpile, 1945 to 1950," *Bulletin of the Atomic Scientists* 38, no. 5 (1982): 25–30.

16. The preventive war question is discussed in William Poundstone, *Prisoner's Dilemma* (New York: Doubleday, 1992), Chapter 7.

17. This is an argument somewhat developed within the U.S. government in the NSC-68 document, of which a declassified version was first published in *Naval War College Review* 27, no. 6 (1975): 51–158.

18. The Eisenhower "considerations" of preventive war are given more weight by Marc Trachtenberg, "A 'Wasting Asset': American Strategy and the Shifting Nuclear Balance," *International Security* 11, no. 3 (1988–1989): 5–49, and less weight in McGeorge Bundy, *Danger and Survival* (New York: Random House, 1985), 251–253.

19. Pierre Gallois, *The Balance of Terror* (Boston: Houghton Mifflin, 1961).

20. On the continuing credibility of U.S. nuclear escalation, see Bernard Brodie, *Escalation and the Nuclear Option* (Princeton, N.J.: Princeton University Press, 1966).

21. For an overview of such theories, see Morton Halperin, *Limited War in the Nuclear Age* (New York: Wiley, 1963).

22. See A. J. Wohlstetter et al., *Selection and Use of Strategic Air Bases* (R-266) (Santa Monica, Calif.: RAND Corporation, 1954).

23. In addition to Gavin, *War and Peace*, see Maxwell Taylor, *The Uncertain Trumpet* (New York: Harper, 1960), and John Medaris, *Countdown for Decision* (New York: Putnam, 1960).

24. The importance of the U-2 and subsequent satellite reconnaissance is outlined in Philip Klass, *Secret Sentries in Space* (New York: Random House, 1971).

25. On the crucial importance of crisis stability, see Thomas C. Schelling and Morton H. Halperin, *Strategy and Arms Control* (New York: Twentieth Century Fund, 1961).

26. The dangers of such a preemptive confrontation are outlined in Herbert Scoville, *MX: Prescription for Disaster* (Cambridge: MIT Press, 1981).

27. An example of this kind of reasoning can be found in Paul Nitze, "Assuring Strategic Stability in an Era of Detente," *Foreign Affairs* 54 (1976): 207–232.

28. The American advantage in the 1980s in submarine and antisubmarine warfare is described in Richard Garwin, "Will Strategic Submarines be Vulnerable?" *International Security* 8, no. 2 (1983): 52–67.

29. The overall impact of the American SDI investment is surveyed by Michael Krepon, "Are Missile Defenses MAD?" *Foreign Affairs* 74 (1995): 19–24.

30. Such a positive interpretation of Reagan's defense expenditures can be found in John Lewis Gaddis, "Hanging Tough Paid Off," *Bulletin of the Atomic Scientists* 45, no. 1 (1989): 11–14.

31. The Bush initiatives are surveyed in Steven E. Miller, "Dismantling the Edifice: Strategic Nuclear Forces in the Post-Soviet Era," in *American Defense Annual*, 9th ed., ed. Charles Hermann (New York: Lexington Books, 1994), 65–84.

32. Additional discussion of the American conventional advantages can be found in Steven Biddle, "U.S. Forces in Europe," in Hermann, *American Defense Annual*, 85–103.

33. On the Russian move toward flexible response, see Wolfgang Panofsky and George Bunn, "The Doctrine of the Nuclear-Weapons States and the Future of Non-Proliferation," *Arms Control Today* 24, no. 6 (1994): 6.

34. A useful survey of the progress of nuclear proliferation can be found in Leonard Spector, *Nuclear Ambitions* (Boulder, Colo.: Westview Press, 1990).

35. On the more altruistic, less power-oriented explanations for the American commitment to nonproliferation, see Joseph Nye, "Maintaining a Non-Proliferation Regime," *International Organization* 35 (1981): 15–30.

2

Rethinking Deterrence: A New Logic to Meet Twenty-First Century Challenges

Lewis A. Dunn

For nearly five decades deterrence was at the center of U.S. national security policy. Initially, deterrence via the threat of nuclear punishment was seen as the most critical means to implement the Cold War policy of containment of Soviet aggression in Europe. Over time, mutual nuclear deterrence between the United States and the former Soviet Union came to be viewed as the key to containing the threat of mutual nuclear devastation. Over those decades U.S. officials periodically debated and redefined the requirements of stable nuclear deterrence, while putting in place a robust set of theater and strategic nuclear and nonnuclear military capabilities designed to convince their Soviet counterparts of the fearful damage that would result from aggression. With the end of the Cold War, the collapse of the former Soviet Union, and the emergence of hostile proliferators armed with chemical or biological weapons (CBW), or possibly even nuclear weaponry, it is timely—and necessary—to begin to rethink in three important respects the role and requirements of deterrence in American security policy.

First, while nuclear weapons continue to provide a hedge against a breakdown of the slow process of political reform in Russia, the logic of nuclear deterrence could well impede rather than support the emergence and regularization of a more cooperative U.S.–Russian political–military relationship. Instead, the logic of mutual nuclear deterrence needs to be first complemented, then gradually subordinated to, and possibly even eventually replaced by a new logic of U.S.–Russian mutual strategic reassurance.

Second, deterrence is and will remain an important element of the overall U.S. posture to contain the new threat to our security and that of our allies and friends posed by hostile countries armed with nuclear, biological, or chemical weapons (NBC)—and means of delivering them in the region or against the American homeland. Nonetheless, some of the most critical canons or mechanisms of traditional Cold War deterrence of Soviet aggression will need to be modified or even set aside in putting in place a new deterrence posture aimed at this proliferation threat. One important element of traditional deterrence, however, will retain its importance, if in a somewhat changed manner: the search for options in answer to the question, "What if deterrence fails?"

Third, faced with growing concern about the danger posed to American society by use of chemical, biological, or perhaps even nuclear weaponry by subnational or terrorist groups, it is important to consider whether there is any role for deterrence—not nuclear deterrence but deterrence by other means—in helping to contain this threat. For the most part, however, recent attention has focused on consequence management, and to a lesser extent prevention of incidents involving nuclear, chemical, or biological weapons. Deterring terrorist or subnational use has been essentially dismissed out of hand. This may be faulty logic.

DETERRENCE, REASSURANCE, AND AN EVOLVING U.S.–RUSSIAN STRATEGIC RELATIONSHIP

Consider first the need to complement and gradually subordinate a logic of mutual deterrence in the U.S.–Russian strategic relationship with a newer logic of mutual strategic reassurance. There are several reasons to be concerned that an exclusive reliance on the logic, analytic assumptions, and habits of thinking of Cold War mutual nuclear deterrence—both here and in Moscow—may well prove counterproductive to the creation of a more cooperative longer-term political and military relationship that we seek with Russia. By definition, thinking in terms of mutual deterrence highlights the conflictual rather than the potentially cooperative aspects of U.S.–Russian relations. The logic of mutual deterrence also focuses attention on residual nuclear capabilities rather than on the great political and military changes that have so reshaped today's security environment—not least the end of the Cold War military confrontation in the heart of Europe. Psychologically, this logic makes it more difficult in both countries to make the mental shift to no longer viewing each other as enemies, despite the fact that until the Bolsheviks seized power in 1917 the two countries had good relations and there is no inherent reason why they should clash in the future.

Operationally, exclusive reliance on the logic of Cold War mutual deterrence in the post–Cold War world has more practical impacts. Russian concern to maintain a robust nuclear deterrent against a future American threat all but certainly partly explains Moscow's rigid affirmation of the 1972 Anti-Ballistic Missile (ABM) Treaty as the foundation for strategic stability and its concomitant reluctance to accept the legitimacy of U.S. theater or limited national missile-defense programs. This is so despite the fact that for the foreseeable future Russia's residual strategic nuclear capabilities would be able to wreak vast destruction on the United States. Unstated U.S. concerns about preserving deterrent flexibility may partly have led to Washington's reluctance to countenance more formal guarantees to Russia that NATO's nuclear weapons would not be moved eastward, though there clearly are no intentions to do so. One consequence was to worsen the political impact of NATO enlargement. On both sides, a too narrow and mechanistic commitment to long-accepted deterrence requirements could well slow and delay a negotiated restructuring of both sides' nuclear postures. Within the United States, for example, uneasiness about Russian proposed numbers of 1,500 deployed strategic nuclear warheads partly reflects a concern about how to do deterrence differently than it has been practiced for the past decades.

Nonetheless, it is most assuredly unrealistic—and quite possibly premature—to propose that the traditional logic of deterrence simply be set aside as the guiding framework for the U.S.–Russian nuclear relationship now. Neither Washington nor Moscow is ready to treat the other side's nuclear potential in a manner comparable to how the United States deals with the nuclear potential of either France or the United Kingdom—in effect, as an afterthought at best.

Nor is this surprising. For the foreseeable future Russia's nuclear arsenal alone will have the technical capability to destroy American society—and vice versa. In turn, for at least the next couple of decades Russian political, economic, and social institutions will be in a period of uncertain transition. It is hoped that the outcome of this great transition will be a more open, democratic, and market-oriented Russia, one that can play a constructive part in both European and global affairs. But that result is not assured. From Russia's perspective the ultimate impact of NATO enlargement on its security remains an equally important uncertainty. This is all the more unsettling because of Moscow's apparent suspicions that the real ambition of the West is to deny Russia the status of even one among several great powers and not to accept its integration into a cooperative framework.

Mutual Strategic Reassurance

What is feasible now—and desirable—is to begin to construct a logic of mutual strategic reassurance as a complement to the logic of mutual nuclear deterrence. This has several dimensions.

At the level of high politics, mutual strategic reassurance requires a practical commitment on the parts of both Washington and Moscow to take actions to enhance security cooperation and to lessen residual suspicions. The successful renegotiation in 1999 of the Conventional Forces in Europe Treaty may be a step in this direction. Greater use can also be made of existing forums for dialogue (e.g., the Permanent Joint Consultative Forum created in conjunction with NATO enlargement). In this area, however, U.S. readiness to work with Russia (and Russia's readiness to work with the United States) to find a mutually acceptable compromise to permit limited U.S. national missile defense against very small proliferator threats within the constraints of a continued if amended ABM Treaty may be the most important action.

On a different level, the logic of mutual strategic reassurance suggests that even more than future nuclear reductions, heightened nuclear transparency should be the centerpiece of the next decade's U.S.–Russian nuclear-arms-control agenda. Within the realm of what is feasible, the purpose of such transparency would be to gradually provide more detailed information about each side's Cold War nuclear legacies: holdings of both weapons and materials. It also would be aimed at opening up the budgets, planning, and decision-making processes on each side. In so doing, windows would be opened into mutual nuclear intentions as well.

The record in the 1990s, however, of U.S.–Russian nuclear transparency is mixed. In practice, U.S. programs to assist Russia under the Cooperative Threat Reduction program as well as to enhance controls on Russian nuclear materials under the Materials Protection Control and Accounting program have resulted in more Americans on more Russian sites than could have been conceived a decade earlier. But more formal transparency negotiations (e.g., to exchange classified nuclear data or on monitored dismantlement of nuclear warheads), have met with difficulties. Success has been impeded by many factors, including traditional Russian secrecy, domestic politics in both countries, and the very logic of mutual deterrence itself with its concern that greater transparency could reveal nuclear vulnerabilities.

These efforts to conclude agreements should continue. At the same time, it may be desirable to step back to look at the longer-term goals. In that regard, one approach would be to set up a high-level U.S.–Russian Joint Working Group on 2010 Transparency Goals and Experiments. Its purpose would be to define on paper what would be the elements of a "cradle to grave" nuclear transparency—comprised of exchanges of data, reciprocal visits, the reciprocal stationing of military personnel at key strategic commands and sites, joint seminars, and joint R&D projects. This group could also identify possible experiments that might be pursued to test given approaches. In that manner, neither side would commit itself irrevocably but both sides would gain insights into each other's activities.

Still another dimension of mutual strategic reassurance would be the identification and pursuit of operational changes in the U.S. and Russian nuclear force postures consistent with that objective. Here, considerable attention has been focused publicly on proposals for so-called dealerting of elements of each side's nuclear forces as a means of moving back from the rapid-response nuclear capabilities of the Cold War era. Some analysts respond that the very different nuclear forces and operating procedures of U.S. and Russian nuclear forces make this step impractical. Others express concerns that dealerting would lead inexorably to declines in force readiness, operational effectiveness, and personnel morale, with eventual implications for the safety and security of residual forces as well. Here, too, one possible next step could be to propose establishment of a joint commission of serving U.S. and Russian military representatives to assess the dealerting concept as well as to identify what other, if any, operational steps might be practicable to shift both sides' nuclear forces toward more standby than rapid response postures.

As already noted, some of these measures that would come under a logic of strategic reassurance have met with resistance, among the U.S. and the Russian nuclear establishments. But language and terminology— how the two sides think and speak within each other as well as with the other side—matters. In that respect, a U.S. and Russian readiness to buy into the need to go beyond traditional deterrence thinking in defining their evolving strategic relationship may be as important as any initial results. Consciously taking mutual strategic reassurance as a guidepost might make it easier to make some forward progress and would itself stimulate new thinking about what actions might be jointly taken. Moreover, a U.S. readiness to seek ways to make it "worth the while"—financially or otherwise—of key Russian bureaucratic players like MINATOM and the ministry of defense to go down this path could help here as it has in other nuclear negotiations since the end of the Cold War.

DETERRENCE AND THE PROLIFERATION CHALLENGE

From Libya in North Africa through Iraq and Iran in the Persian Gulf to North Korea in Northeast Asia, the United States confronts hostile countries either seeking or already in possession of chemical, biological, or nuclear weapons. For these new proliferators the threat or actual employment of such weapons could be intended to serve many purposes.

In the opening stages of a future Gulf crisis or confrontation, for example, implied or explicit CBW threats might be used by Iraq as a means to undermine the political resolve of the United States, its regional friends, and possible outside coalition partners. In that regard, threats to the American homeland cannot be ruled out. Or either North Korean or Iraqi use of biological or chemical weapons in the early stages of a conflict against key ports, airfields, and logistics nodes could be aimed at disrupting the flow of U.S. and coalition forces into the theater. Still another possibility is that desperate last-resort use of a nuclear weapon against South Korea or Japan—with the implicit threat of additional use—could be seen by Pyongyang as the only means to bring to a halt a U.S.–ROK (Republic of Korea) counteroffensive across the DMZ in the closing stages of a second Korean War.

A robust deterrent posture is now and will remain the first line of defense for U.S. and coalition military forces against these types of new proliferation threats. A credible deterrent posture is also essential to maintain host-nation support and coalition unity. Nonetheless, some of the key canons, approaches, or mechanisms of traditional Cold War deterrence of Soviet blackmail or aggression may need to be modified or even set aside in designing a new deterrent posture aimed at hostile proliferators. Specifically, this includes all of the following key aspects of traditional Cold War deterrence:

- High confidence in the target of deterrent threats and retaliatory responses.
- An explicit reliance on the threat of nuclear punishment.
- A rejection of deterrence by denial, including a rejection of active and passive defenses as either destabilizing or ineffective, or both.
- A high premium placed on avoiding limited incidents or any direct military confrontation between the two sides' military forces.
- Heavy reliance on formal institutions for coalition maintenance and intra-alliance reassurance in the face of the NBC threat.

That said, there also is likely to be one great carryover from Cold War deterrence: a search for a full range of response options in answer to the question "What if deterrence fails?" Let me touch briefly on each of these elements.

"Whodunit"—and Did They?

During the Cold War the subject of U.S. deterrent strategy—and the target of U.S. retaliation—was very clear. It was the former Soviet Union. Despite occasional speculation about so-called catalytic wars, there was little serious doubt that if nuclear weapons were used against U.S. forces or the American homeland. Moscow would have been the user. Nor was there any question that if a nuclear weapon was used, we would have known it.

Though both propositions probably remain valid in thinking about deterrence of nuclear weapons use by hostile proliferators, neither may be valid for the more troubling challenge of deterring use of biological weapons (BW). Chemical weapons use may fall in-between. Specifically, clandestine employment or ambiguous threats of BW use might be seen by a hostile proliferator (e.g., an Iraq in a future Gulf clash), as a means to hide its hand. If successful, we would not know against whom to retaliate. Even if we had suspicions, such clandestine use could greatly complicate a U.S. decision to retaliate, or at the least shape the nature of U.S. retaliation. Or in such a clash involving U.S. and Iraqi forces, a hostile Iran could well contemplate covert use of BW as a means to catalyze U.S. retaliation against Iraq. It would gamble that Iraq would be blamed. In turn, a hostile proliferator might seek to use biological weapons in a manner that mimicked a natural outbreak of disease. In so doing, its leaders would hope to deflect or constrain U.S. retaliation by raising sufficient doubts about whether BW had even been used.

To counter the possibility of attempted ambiguous use of BW, timely, accurate, and releasable intelligence will be especially important. Near-real-time forensics to determine that BW had been used and to characterize an attack will also be critical. Signaling such capabilities to potential BW users would heighten the prospects for successful deterrence.

The Role of Nuclear Threats

An explicit threat of devastating nuclear punishment was at the heart of Cold War deterrence, whether of a direct nuclear attack on the American homeland or of Warsaw Pact aggression across the intra-German border. Great pains were taken over the Cold War decades by U.S. defense planners to make that threat credible, both in Soviet eyes and in the eyes of U.S. allies. This entailed, for example, the steps in the 1950s to ensure a survivable second-strike capability through the implementation of flexible response, the search for limited nuclear options in the 1960s and 1970s, and the hard-fought but successful deployments of intermediate-range nuclear systems in the 1980s. Throughout, U.S. and NATO doctrine included the threat of first use of nuclear weapons.

The threat of nuclear retaliation continues to have a role to play in deterring use of nuclear weapons by a hostile proliferator. Few persons would deny this. By contrast, the role of threats of nuclear punishment in deterring the use of biological or chemical weapons already is a subject of growing controversy. Several considerations need to be weighed in thinking through this issue.

Given the potentially awesome destructiveness of nuclear weapons, a credible threat of nuclear retaliation is likely to have the most psychological impact on the leadership of countries like Iraq, Iran, and North Korea. In that regard, public comments by Iraqi officials after the Gulf War affirm that Saddam's fear of a U.S. nuclear reprisal played an important part in Iraq's decision not to use CBW. Though these statements may be intended to serve some other purpose, as some persons have suggested, they also cannot be dismissed. Moreover, for leaders that have already chosen to go to war despite the prospect of conventional military losses, the threat of conventional military punishment may be considerably less compelling. Indeed, if Desert Shield is typical, U.S. and coalition air power may already be inflicting very high damage on the proliferator's military, technical, and industrial infrastructure.

Nonetheless, under some conditions an explicit threat of nuclear punishment in response to CBW use may lack credibility. This may be especially so in response to more limited or ambiguous uses of either biological or chemical weapons in which the loss of life is very low although the political and military significance may be fairly high. Clandestine use of nonlethal BW agents to disrupt port operations that depend on civilian workers or to coerce a host country are two possibilities. Faced with more limited or ambiguous use, moreover, pressure would likely be high from coalition partners, regional neighbors, and domestic publics that nuclear weapons not be used in response. Further, legitimate concerns about the long-term precedent set by the first use of nuclear weapons in over five decades could be expected to raise doubts among senior U.S. decision makers about a nuclear reprisal in anything short of the most extreme circumstances.

The political and international costs of explicit reliance on the threat of nuclear punishment to deter CBW use already are high—and likely to grow higher over time. Both unilaterally and under several treaties creating nuclear-weapon-free zones, the United States has already made a commitment not to use nuclear weapons against nonnuclear-weapon states unless those states are engaged in an armed conflict in alliance with a nuclear-weapon state. Key U.S. allies in both the Gulf and northeast Asia, moreover, could be expected to take issue with too open a reliance on nuclear threats in deterring CBW use, even against them.

Taken together, these competing considerations suggest that it would be imprudent to rule out the possibility of a nuclear response to particularly egregious uses of CBW. But it would be equally imprudent to rely explicitly or exclusively on the threat of nuclear punishment for CBW deterrence. The threat of nuclear punishment may best be kept in the background, casting its shadow but not dominating the scene.

New Look at Active and Passive Defenses

Turning to a closely related element of traditional deterrence, early discussions in the 1950s of the possibility of deterrence by denial quickly were supplanted by the emphasis on deterrence by the threat of punishment. In turn, the logic of Cold War nuclear deterrence rejected pursuit of active defenses and passive defenses as either ineffectual or destabilizing, or both.

By contrast, particularly for deterrence of CBW use by hostile proliferators, active and passive defenses—denial measures—have an important contribution to make to an overall deterrence posture. A wide range of programmatic capabilities is currently being pursued. These include theater missile defenses, enhanced early warning of CBW use, next-generation CBW protective gear, preparations and workarounds to deal with the impact of use, improved medical responses, and vaccination of U.S. forces.

Effective active and passive CBW defenses would enhance deterrence in three ways. They would influence a potential proliferator's assessment of whether use of CBW would reap the desired military or political gains. At the same time, enhanced denial capabilities would raise the threshold for potentially effective CBW use. This would in turn require a proliferator to take more extreme actions and run a greater risk of triggering the use of extreme measures in retaliation. Not least, a readiness to take certain high-visibility steps—for instance, a decision to vaccinate all U.S. forces against anthrax—would itself signal U.S. resolve to deny hostile proliferators whatever gains they seek from CBW threats or use.

Two related political as opposed to technical soft spots of enhanced denial efforts, however, need to be stressed. These are the vulnerabilities of host-nation civilians and U.S. coalition partners, respectively. Unless those vulnerabilities are addressed, a hostile proliferator might well conclude that use of CBW could lead to significant political or even military advantages.

Military Responses to Lesser Provocations

Still another canon of the Cold War deterrence relationship between the United States and the former Soviet Union was the assumption that there was a high risk that any direct military clash between their military forces could run out of control and escalate to a society-devastating nuclear war. For that reason, both Washington and Moscow sought to avoid low-level incidents and limited military clashes between them. At the same time, a wide range of nonmilitary actions were relied on to show resolve, demonstrate commitments, and signal seriousness of intentions.

Contrasted with this Cold War situation, the risks of confrontation and lesser military clashes short of war with hostile proliferators are considerably less for the United States. Avoiding any use of force no longer must be considered a guiding precept. To the contrary, rather than being a potential trigger of a breakdown of deterrence, limited uses of military power in situations short of war may be a critical means to buttress deterrence of hostile proliferators.

Put otherwise, how the United States responds to lesser provocations by such countries—typified, for instance, by Iraq's violation of the "no-fly" and "no-drive" zones or by Iranian support for terrorism—may be especially important. Those responses will be one of the main determinants of proliferators' perceptions of U.S. resolve and, in turn, of the risks of using nuclear, biological, or chemical weapons in a clash with U.S. and coalition forces. Weak responses, which do little if any lasting damage to what the leaders of these proliferators and their close supporters value, all but certainly would send the wrong signal. No responses would be even worse. Instead, a focus on long-term deterrence considerations would suggest purposefully, if selectively, targeting high-value assets in such situations.

Coalition Reassurance by Other Means

Still another essential element of U.S. Cold War deterrence in Europe was its institutionalization. Within the basic framework provided by the NATO treaty, there grew over the decades a mixture of an extensive American military and civilian presence, forward nuclear deployments, and formal consultative mechanisms, including NATO's Nuclear Planning Group. Taken together, these institutions visibly demonstrated the American nuclear guarantee and provided needed reassurance to our European allies. As such, they also played a critical role in maintaining the alliance's solidarity in the face of Soviet power.

With regard to deterrence of proliferator NBC use, a considerable American military but not civilian presence is likely to remain a defining feature in both Asia and the Gulf. But most of the other mechanisms for institutionalizing deterrence and reassuring friends are unlikely to prove transferable outside of Europe.

For instance, there is little prospect of the deployment of American tactical nuclear weapons to South Korea or Japan as a means of signaling North Korea that its use of NBC weaponry against either country could trigger nuclear escalation. Similarly, within the Gulf region there all but certainly would be little interest in either the type of forward deployments or routinized nuclear consultations that characterized extended nuclear deterrence in Europe.

Set aside the question of whether this change is good or bad. Take it as a given. We shall need to find and rely on other mechanisms to provide reassurance to friends and allies threatened with NBC weaponry. We shall need other means to create and nurture sufficient patterns of cooperation to withstand implicit or explicit NBC threats by hostile proliferators. In that regard, it may be especially important to build on recent efforts to put in place a wider pattern of cooperation in enhanced defenses and denial capabilities—not only with our NATO allies but with others. Routinized consultations on the defense-planning proliferation challenge will also be valuable. Here, too, responses to lesser provocations may play an important part not simply in influencing hostile proliferators' calculations but in reassuring nervous friends and allies. Not least, as in the NATO alliance, ensuring a strong network of cooperation across the spectrum of political–military issues prior to any crisis or confrontation involving a hostile proliferator will be critical.

What If Deterrence Fails?

Beginning in the 1960s, U.S. defense decision makers sought repeatedly to expand the retaliatory options open to the president in the event of conflict with the Soviet Union beyond defeat or large-scale nuclear use. "No cities," flexible response, limited nuclear options, nuclear withholds, and selective nuclear options were but a few of the incarnations under which this search for options was repeatedly pursued.

The search for options will remain an important—if changed—dimension of post–Cold War deterrence of hostile proliferators for a number of reasons. In response to more limited or ambiguous uses of chemical or biological weapons, for instance, the threat of nuclear response may not be credible. Moreover, international political costs and the possible longer-term implications of breaking the nuclear nonuse threshold would argue against a nuclear response if at all possible. This would likely remain so following more extreme uses of biological weapons resulting in significant U.S. military or civilian fatalities. Even in the aftermath of an isolated use of a nuclear weapon by a hostile proliferator, concern for long-term global order in a world of nuclear weapons might well argue against a nuclear response—or at least argue for a highly tailored response.

Ensuring that the president has the fullest possible set of response options in the event that deterrence breaks down and nuclear, biological, or chemical weapons are used, however, will be a tough task. Questions abound.

Given an ongoing intense conventional conflict, what additional conventional response options would really be available? Would any such options entail conventional escalation to attacks on civilian populations or civilian economic infrastructure, despite the fact that the civilians would likely have had little to do with a decision to use NBC? How might a nuclear weapon or nuclear weapons be used in retaliation; in what number, against what targets, for what purpose, within what set of political, military, and legal guidelines? In particular, if nuclear weapons are used, how could they be used to terminate the war as quickly as possible? Are there any nonnuclear, nontraditional responses that might be pursued? In particular, is there a way to put teeth in the oft-heard remark that the U.S. response, especially to BW use, should be to make the proliferator an international outlaw, bringing down the country's regime and punishing its leaders? Has the time arrived to rethink and change existing legislative restraints on U.S. actions against such leaders? Do we need a posture of holding leaders accountable for the use of chemical and biological weapons?

Asking what happens if deterrence fails raises one further issue—particularly with regard to the threat posed by biological weapons in the hands of hostile proliferators. Throughout the Cold War biological weapons were never used, with the possible exception of the still highly controversial alleged use of mycotoxins—so-called yellow rain—in southeast Asia. The first modern-day use of biological weapons will be as seminal and defining an event as was the first use of atomic weapons at Hiroshima and Nagasaki. That use—and especially how the international community responds—will greatly affect countries' perceptions of the risks and benefits, uses and usability of BW.

Working with other countries, U.S. leadership is needed to ensure that the country that next uses BW not only does not achieve its objectives but that its leaders pay a high price. Failure to do so will only encourage additional uses, making deterrence all the more difficult. Success in setting an example of the first BW user will send a very different signal, buttressing deterrence and comprising the first step to a nonuse rule. This does not mean that we need to act alone, or that we need to respond instantaneously. Nor is this a call for a nuclear response. But given the international magnitude of the event, it is none too soon to begin consulting with close allies to seek a consensus that the next user of BW will not go unpunished.

THE SUBNATIONAL DIMENSION: WHAT ROLE FOR DETERRENCE?

Turning to the third proposition about the future of deterrence, is it necessary to give greater thought to the potential role of deterrence as a complement to prevention and consequence management in helping to meet the challenge of NBC terrorism? As suggested by the actions of the Japanese Aum Shinrikyo group, including its release of both sarin and anthrax in Tokyo, there is sufficient reason to be concerned about possible NBC terrorist acts—especially with chemical or biological weapons, but also with a radiological weapon or an improvised nuclear device. In addition, access to the materials and technology needed to produce and disseminate biological or chemical weapons—and, to a lesser degree, to produce a radiological or nuclear weapon—is becoming increasingly widespread. Given these assumptions, what types of groups or organizations might contemplate NBC terrorism? Would they be deterrable? By what?

Recent experience suggests that a very wide range of subnational or terrorists groups might contemplate NBC terrorism—and for very different reasons. We could confront, for instance, any of the following: A "pick-up" terrorist group of a handful of individuals, whether motivated by religion like the perpetrators of the World Trade Center bombing or by right-wing ideology like the Texas Militia. Their purpose could be to cause death and destruction, to strike out and punish a hated authority. Or the terrorist group might be a rejectionist political organization, like Hamas or Hezbollah. Either of these groupings could view use of CBW as a last-resort means to disrupt and head off a future political settlement in the Middle East that it found unacceptable.

What about the violent wing of a well-organized and ruthless revolutionary movement? It might regard use of CBW as part of a well-thought-out strategy to create political repression and chaos, which could be exploited by its nonviolent wing to bring down the government in a democratic liberal society. Still another possibility is a well-organized, well-financed, and somewhat technically advanced fringe movement, like Japan's Aum Shinrikyo. It appears to have had plans to use CBW terrorism as a means to kill senior Japanese officials, create a power vacuum, and then, without knowing how it would do so, take advantage of the chaos to seize power.

One final possibility, itself linked to several of the preceding terrorist profiles, should not be overlooked. This is a state-sponsored terrorist group, like the Libyans who bombed the Berlin disco in 1986, or a decade later, the group that bombed Khobar Towers in Saudi Arabia. In one case revenge, in the other a desire to raise the price on the U.S. presence in the Gulf appear to have been the motivations.

Deterrable by What?

For at least several of these groups, an NBC terrorist act—or for that matter, other lesser acts of terrorism—would likely entail a carefully weighed political decision. It would reflect a balancing of the perceived benefits of using NBC against potential costs of doing so. They also would consider the costs of not resorting to an NBC terrorist action; that is, of letting the existing state of affairs continue or using other means. This applies, for instance, to Hamas or Hezbollah or some future IRA-like revolutionary organization. These same groups also tend to be well organized, with established structures and bases of operation and identifiable leaderships. Though prepared to recruit and use suicide bombers, those leaders give no suggestion of having a death wish themselves. For them, deterrence could conceivably be brought to bear. In particular, in their case not only would they weigh the costs and benefits of use but they also would have other means to pursue their objectives. By contrast, deterrence seems likely to have little if any role to play in the case of an ad hoc grouping of disgruntled individuals bent on destruction and prepared to lose their lives in the process.

What sorts of deterrent actions might warrant more extensive assessment? Enhanced measures to prevent a subnational group from carrying out a terrorist incident, if known, could have a limited deterrent impact by affecting perceptions of the odds of success. More effective protection and consequence management, though necessary, could be a two-edged sword. By reducing the impact of CBW use, such actions could paradoxically lessen its perceived adverse political costs and paradoxically make terrorism appear more, not less, attractive.

But the heart of any attempt to bring deterrence to bear in meeting the NBC terrorist threat would have to be a credible threat of punishment. To that end, we could make clear that the United States considers acts of NBC terrorism against American nationals to cross a red line. Once crossed, we would accept no restraints in pursuing NBC terrorists and exacting the highest price for their actions. In effect, we could follow Israel's example in dealing generally with terrorism, an approach which many counterterrorism experts believe has helped contain but not preclude terrorist actions against that state.

Reliance on the threat of punishment to deter terrorist use of NBC weaponry clearly would raise tough issues and painful choices. Unless it is possible to identify the perpetrator, we may not know whom to punish. In some, though not necessarily a majority, of situations ascribing responsibility may be very difficult. Innocent lives may also be unintentionally put at risk. For those terrorist leaders who might be deterrable, the most compelling punitive threat could well be fear of direct personal retribution. Carrying out such a threat would run counter to existing executive-mandated restraints and clash with long-standing American values. Nonetheless, for their part, the American people may demand no less after a particularly egregious act of NBC terrorism.

It is, of course, not possible here to resolve this question of what role can deterrence play—and how—in helping to contain the challenge of NBC terrorism. Even this brief treatment, however, suggests that a more extensive assessment and debate is in order about the potential benefits, risks, and implications of threats of punitive retaliation as part of a counter-NBC-terrorist posture.

CONCLUSION

Deterrence has been and in many ways remains the centerpiece of U.S. national security strategy. It has been the subject of an extensive academic and think-tank literature, as well as of intensive study, debate, and planning within the U.S. government and the American military. Other countries, as well, have oriented their national-security thinking in terms of precepts of deterrence—some adapted from the United States, others developed independently. As the twenty-first century unfolds it is increasingly important to rethink this deterrence legacy. Parts of it remain valid, other parts need to be amended and revised, still other elements could hinder and not support evolution toward a more stable global political order in the post–Cold War world. This chapter is intended to help serve that process of revamping deterrence to meet the challenges of the coming century.

NOTE

The views expressed in this chapter are those of the author, not necessarily of Science Applications International Corporation or any of its sponsoring agencies.

3

Post–Cold War Nuclear Scenarios: Implications for a New Strategic Calculus

James Scouras

The context for strategic arms control has changed profoundly due to the end of the Cold War and the dissolution of the Soviet Union, and continues to evolve in response to the proliferation of weapons of mass destruction and advances in ballistic missile defense technology. Although recognition of this new strategic environment has resulted in significant changes in strategic force structure, posture, and doctrine, and a START III treaty may be on the horizon, further change is likely to prove increasingly difficult and the long-range goals of strategic arms control remain contentious. The continuing uncertain prospects for entry into force of the START II Treaty, the U.S. Senate rejection of the Comprehensive Test Ban Treaty, and U.S. attempts to gain Russian acquiescence on modification of the ABM Treaty are warnings that the tapestry of arms control agreements woven over some three decades may be unraveling. Under these circumstances, the need to reassess the long-term U.S. interests in strategic arms control is imperative.

Critical decisions loom on the deployment of national missile defenses and the framework, objectives, and negotiating strategy for a START III agreement, options that may well prove mutually exclusive. In the intermediate and longer term the United States faces such issues as deterring, preempting, and responding to chemical and biological as well as nuclear attacks by rogue nations and substate actors; maintaining a reliable nuclear arsenal in the absence of nuclear weapon testing; possible multilateralization of strategic arms control; the relationships among nuclear warfare and other forms of strategic warfare; the wisdom of dealerting strategic forces; further modifying declaratory strategy and employment doctrine; and defining a stable nuclear end state for the planet.

One particularly important but little-examined source of difficulty in engaging and resolving these issues is that Cold War methods of analysis and measures of effectiveness are of uncertain relevance in this new era. The Cold War afforded the relative simplicity of a two-player game dominated by a single nuclear war scenario—a massive Soviet attack on the United States followed by a U.S. retaliation—that provided a cohesive analytical structure for evaluating both the utility of strategic forces and the arms control agreements that sought to constrain them. Other scenarios and variants were considered, but only secondarily and as subordinate cases. That is, if U.S. strategic forces were adequate against a massive attack by the Soviet Union, they also would serve, with appropriate changes in employment doctrine, to deter lesser attacks by the Soviet Union (e.g., counterforce attacks) and attacks by China. Theater nuclear forces served primarily to add credibility to the threat of first use, especially in Europe, where NATO feared Warsaw Pact conventional superiority, and to provide a rung in the ladder of escalation.

The central element of U.S. national security strategy during the Cold War was deterrence of an attack on the United States through the threat of unacceptable retaliatory damage. The dominant measure of strategic force effectiveness in underwriting this deterrence strategy was damage expectancy. Damage expectancy evaluated the quality of the U.S. deterrent by assessing the level of retaliatory damage the United States could inflict on targeted installations in the Soviet Union. Toward the latter half of the Cold War, after both sides' arsenals had clearly achieved powerful second-strike capabilities and were beginning to be limited and reduced by the SALT and START treaties, attention focused on the issue of first-strike stability. The concern was that even with devastating second-strike capabilities on both sides, if either side would fare significantly better by striking first rather than second that side could feel pressured to do so in a crisis. Invariably, no matter how devastating the damage to both sides, the side that strikes first does fare better, if only in a relative sense, than it would have fared had the other side struck first, so the issue became how much better? A cottage industry in quantitative measures of first-strike stability developed in the United States to address this question, with the most elaborate developed by Kent and Thaler in 1989.[1]

Now that the Cold War is over, the massive Russian attack scenario and its associated strategic force measures of effectiveness are being challenged as relics of the Cold War. While it is relatively easy, however, to assail "Cold War thinking," it is not so easy to develop new, more relevant analytical approaches. The challenge is to define a methodology—a *strategic calculus*—analogous to that described briefly for the Cold War, which can be employed to evaluate the contribution of strategic forces to U.S. national security. A strategic calculus for the post–Cold War era would provide a structured way of thinking about the diverse strategic arms control issues facing us. It would help us to see the relationships among seemingly disparate issues and, most important, facilitate constructive dialogs between advocates of opposing viewpoints.

Developing a strategic calculus relevant to the post–Cold War era is an ambitious undertaking; this analysis attempts only the first steps. In particular, it addresses the most basic questions:

1. Are nuclear weapons still relevant?
2. Is nuclear deterrence still a relevant strategy, and how should we assess the contribution of strategic forces to underwriting it?
3. Is first-strike stability still a relevant concept, and how should we evaluate it?

This chapter begins by briefly examining three salient features of the post–Cold War strategic environment: the diminution of the Russian threat, the rise of the rogue nation threat, and renewed emphasis on ballistic missile defenses. The analysis then turns to the post–Cold War experience with crises that have involved implicit or explicit nuclear threats or actions, or those in which the simple existence of nuclear weapons has played an important role. In particular, this analysis considers the 1991 coup attempt against Gorbachev and the 1995 Norwegian meteorological rocket launch. The three questions are then addressed in turn and the scenarios further mined for insights into the elements of a post–Cold War strategic calculus.

A word of caution is in order: Developing a strategic calculus is an analytically messy process. This chapter explores the strategic landscape freely, whether or not direct links to a strategic calculus are foreseen. These links may come later, or they may not come at all. No matter. One objective on the road toward a strategic calculus is to provoke thinking by emphasizing those aspects of ongoing debates that have not received their fair share of attention. Once a post–Cold War strategic calculus has been developed, explaining it can be a neat and orderly top-down process, and this author looks forward to that day.

THE POST–COLD WAR STRATEGIC ENVIRONMENT

The post–Cold War era is clearly a period of transition. Its ultimate character is unknown and, as its name suggests, it is defined primarily in contrast to the previous era. While many have described the international order as moving toward multipolarity as opposed to the bipolar Cold War confrontation, the current state of affairs is more accurately characterized as a unipolar world. The United States is unrivaled in the breadth and depth of both economic and military power, with political and cultural influence to match. Many nations recognize this reality and are struggling against it. Russia, for example, takes as a basis for its post–Cold War military doctrine the following assessment of the existing military–political situation:[2]

The status and prospects for the development of the present-day military–political situation are determined by the opposition of two tendencies: on the one hand, a tendency toward establishing a unipolar world based on the domination of one superpower and on the other hand, a tendency toward forming a multipolar world based on the equal rights of peoples and nations, on consideration for and assurance of a balance of the national interests of states, and on implementation of fundamental rules of international law.

The Russian Federation proceeds from the assumption that social progress, stability and international security can be ensured only within the framework of a multipolar world, and *it will assist in its formation in every way possible* [italics added].

Unipolarity may be a transient phase in any event. Dynamic forces at work in economics, technology, military power, international relations, cultural identity, and demographics are shaping the world's near- and far-term futures in ways that can be only dimly seen. But true multipolarity, with several near-equal centers of power, appears a distant possibility.

Fortunately, this analysis can focus on those aspects of the post–Cold War environment that most directly affect U.S. national security, especially as it relates to weapons of mass destruction. In addition, we need not be overly concerned with the highly uncertain distant future. It is challenging enough to try to see things clearly as they are and project for a decade or so. After that, all bets are off.

The Diminution of the Russian Threat

What is it about the post–Cold War strategic environment that should motivate a reevaluation of the ways the contributions of U.S. strategic forces to national security are measured? In particular, why does a massive Russian attack seem so implausible? The generally proffered answer is not that Russia doesn't have the *capability* to mount such an attack, but that because Russia lacks the Soviet *intent* to achieve world domination it no longer sees the United States as its enemy, the principal obstacle to fulfilling its ambitions. Well beyond lack of enmity, the United States is attempting to forge a "strategic partnership," involving a broad spectrum of economic, military, and political cooperation. These links are intended both to foster mutual understanding and to make it in Russia's interest to maintain them; that is, to increase their engagement of and dependency on the West. So, the argument concludes, if Russia has no incentive and even strong disincentives to deliberately attack the United States, there is no possibility of it happening. The only attacks from Russia we have to worry about are relatively small accidental and unauthorized launches.

This logic can be attacked on several fronts, but the most compelling counterarguments involve recognizing that it presupposes a comprehensive understanding of the Russian perspective, implicitly assumes the future will be a straightforward extension of the recent past, and depends on an unwarranted faith in rationality. With regard to the first point, understanding the Russian perspective implies that there is indeed such a thing. As should be evident from even a cursory examination of Russian politics, there is no single, or even clearly dominant, Russian perspective on many issues. Whether the situation will improve under Putin is anyone's guess, but Yeltsin's views often differed from those of his defense and foreign ministers and other key executive-branch members (a rapidly changing group), there was a tension between the prevailing views in the General Staff and the civilian leadership, and competition between the executive branch and the Duma periodically paralyzed the government. Views of individuals do matter and it is not always clear who is in charge or who will be in charge. The leaders we have to face in a crisis may not hold the same views as the civilian political leadership we deal with on a daily basis.

Putting aside the nearly insurmountable difficulties inherent in understanding the decision-making dynamics of complex organizations and the psyches of its members, one underappreciated impediment to discerning Russian perspectives is the natural tendency to mirror image; that is, to project U.S. thinking and U.S. views on others. Since we believe nuclear war is improbable, so too must Russia. Since we perceive that Russia is no longer a threat, it must perceive the same of us. Since we would never contemplate a first strike against Russia, it will never contemplate a first strike against us. U.S. views of Russia's views about the United States may say more about U.S. views of Russia than Russia's views of the United States.

A good starting point for understanding the post–Cold War threat perceptions of at least the Russian military leadership (i.e., the General Staff) and how Russia intends to respond to these threats is the official pronouncement of Russian military doctrine, *Basic Provisions of the Military Doctrine of the Russian Federation*, pushed by the General

Staff, approved by the Russian Federation Security Council, and adopted by presidential edict in November 1993. With respect to both nuclear and conventional attacks, this document codifies the primacy of nuclear deterrence: "The aim of the Russian Federation's policy in the sphere of nuclear weapons is to eliminate the danger of nuclear war by deterring the launching of aggression against the Russian Federation and its allies."[3] A careless reading of this statement would hold that Russia's strategy of deterrence is intended to deter nuclear attack upon Russia. But the statement refers to the "launching of aggression," not nuclear attack, and the objective is to "eliminate the danger of nuclear war," not to eliminate the danger of nuclear attack. Russia's nuclear deterrent is intended to avoid wars that Russia might well turn nuclear. This point becomes clear when the document establishes the conditions under which Russia will not employ nuclear weapons and, by implication, the other situations in which Russia contemplates nuclear use:[4]

The Russian Federation will not employ its nuclear weapons against any state-party to the Treaty on the Nonproliferation of Nuclear Weapons, dated 1 July 1968, which does not possess nuclear weapons except in cases of (a) an armed attack against the Russian Federation, its territory, Armed Forces, other troops, or its allies by any state which is connected by an alliance agreement with a state that does possess nuclear weapons; (b) joint actions by such a state with a state possessing nuclear weapons in the carrying out or in support of any invasion or armed conflict upon the Russian Federation, its territory, Armed Forces, other troops, or its allies.

A rewording of this statement, reinforced by a presentation given by Lieutenant General G. D. Ivanov to U.S. Department of Defense officials in October 1994, is that Russia will rely on conventional, as opposed to nuclear, deterrence only in the difficult-to-imagine case of an aggressor that is a signatory to the Nonproliferation Treaty, that does not possess nuclear weapons, that is not allied to a nuclear state, and that is not acting in concert with or being supported by a nuclear state.[5] In all other cases of a nonnuclear aggressor (i.e., a conventional attack) Russia intends to rely on nuclear deterrence and, if that fails, nuclear response. This is a clear statement of increased reliance on nuclear weapons. It explicitly condones nuclear use in the event of nuclear or conventional aggression over a much broader range of circumstances than envisioned during the Cold War. As Ivanov observes, "Russia's new military doctrine includes a harsher, stricter component in its nuclear policy with respect to surrounding countries. Objectively, the multifaceted nature of new threats to peace justifies this component."[6]

Russia's increased reliance on nuclear weapons is understandable, even inevitable, given its current circumstances. During most of the Cold War the Red Army was the greatest conventional military power in Eurasia. Fear of an invasion of Western Europe drove NATO to deploy theater nuclear weapons in Europe and to develop a detailed employment doctrine for their possible use, including first use. Now U.S. conventional military power is reaching new heights, with precision guided weaponry, stealth technology, and information technology, while Russia can barely feed its troops and maintain internal control, let alone project power. Russia sees a multitude of threats on its periphery that could develop into major conflicts, the most troubling of which may be the potential expansion of NATO to incorporate the Baltic states. Russia's only recourse, at least until her economy can once again support a robust conventional capability, is to rely on nuclear weapons to deter both nuclear and conventional threats, and that is the course she has chosen.[7]

The second counterargument to the logic for dismissing the possibility of a massive Russian attack is based on recognizing that events of the recent past may not be indicative of even the immediate future. The historical record of U.S. failures to foresee the initiation of major wars is particularly dismal. The United States was surprised by the Japanese attack on Pearl Harbor in 1941 and the North Korean invasion of South Korea in 1950, didn't understand the origins of the Vietnam War, and didn't foresee Iraq annexing Kuwait in 1990. This record does not inspire confidence that we will see the next major war coming.

Although history is periodically punctuated by, for all practical purposes, unforeseeable events, it seems that the fine art of prediction invariably assumes that either things will remain as they are or, at best, projects that current trends will continue indefinitely so that the future will be a linear projection of the recent past. So, if U.S.–Russian relations have improved in the immediate past they will continue to do so. If Russia has taken the first steps toward true democracy, the other steps will follow. If Russia hasn't launched a major nuclear attack yet, it never will.

With respect to the forging of a strategic partnership, this author believes that although results to date have been discouraging due to a combination of waste, corruption, and misguided implementation, substantial benefit can still be derived from encouraging Russia to integrate more fully with the West. In fact, this appears to be the only reasonable long-term strategy. However, we must recognize that success in reducing the probability of war requires a very high level of interdependency; otherwise, national imperatives and internal political processes will more likely dominate crisis decision making. As a point of comparison, Germany prior to both world wars was much more heavily invested in nations it attacked than Russia is in the West today and likely to be in the foreseeable future.

The implicit assumption of rationality underlying the Russia-won't-attack school also fails to give proper recognition of the possibility of emotional responses. Emotionalism is a potent political force in Russia today, ranging from Vladimir Zhirinovsky's[8] diatribes on reconstructing the Russian empire (including Alaska!) to General Aleksandr Lebed's[9] hawkish anti-Americanism to Aleksandr Solzhenitsyn's[10] messianic mysticism. Since the end of the Cold War, Russia has lost her satellites, her republics, her society, her wealth, her military might, her status in the world, and her self-respect. This situation is ripe for a demagogue who promises to save Russia (and the world) from the evil United States, source and symbol of all that ails Russia. Two gems from Zhirinovsky and Lebed make this point starkly:

The United States is an empire of evil, the nucleus of hell, which is behind the beginning of every war. (Vladimir Zhirinovsky, February 1993)

The Soviet conscience, still borne by many of our citizens, leaves no room for doubt. They wonder, "Who is responsible for our disintegration?" China? No. The Islamic world? No. Who then? The West. (General Aleksandr Lebed, March 1996)

Even if we accept that Russia does not have and never will have any incentive to deliberately attack the United States, it does not follow that it won't happen. Crises have minds of their own and can spin out of control to thwart the intentions of all parties involved. The classic example of this is, of course, World War I, the origins of which can be traced to the assassination of Archduke Franz Ferdinand in Sarajevo in 1914, an essentially trivial event that, by all reason, should have remained a footnote in history. More recently, neither Kennedy nor Khrushchev wanted the Cuban missile crisis to result in a nuclear war, but neither felt confident in his ability to avert this catastrophic end to the crisis. Keith Payne's analysis of deterrence provides numerous additional examples of the fragility of deterrence and the unpredictability of crises.[11]

All this is to make the case that the possibility of a massive Russian attack should not be dismissed in the post–Cold War era. This does not mean that such an attack is probable; in fact, it is probably highly improbable under current circumstances. But so are all nuclear war scenarios. We are dealing with a low-likelihood but extremely high-consequence event for which neither the likelihood is well known nor the consequences completely comprehensible. We could ask whether such an attack is less probable or more probable than other avenues to nuclear war, but there is obviously no data on the future with which to resolve the question. For purposes of this analysis, we need only determine that a massive Russian attack is not so improbable that we can safely relegate it to the back burner. That the massive Russian attack scenario should be included in a U.S. post–Cold War strategic calculus, however, does not imply that it should be the only scenario. Unlike during the Cold War, other possibilities should not be treated as subordinate cases.

The Rise of the Rogue Nation Threat

A second salient feature of the post–Cold War strategic environment is increasing U.S. concern with the emerging threat from rogue nations armed with weapons of mass destruction. The pejorative term "rogue nation" appears to apply to states that (1) are not major powers, (2) are generally hostile to the United States, (3) have ambitions to influence events beyond their borders, (4) (optionally) engage in terrorist activities, and, most important, (5) are attempting to acquire weapons of mass destruction. This select club is currently comprised of North Korea, Iran, Iraq, and Libya, although others may meet the membership requirements at any time. What characterizes these nations, according to the United States, is that they don't play by established norms for international conduct.[12] As U.S. concern with Russia has diminished, rightly or wrongly, the perceived threat posed by these rogue nations has expanded to fill the vacuum.

Not surprisingly, the threat from rogue nations becomes especially worrisome as they acquire the capability to directly threaten the United States with weapons of mass destruction. The delivery system of greatest concern is the intercontinental ballistic missile, although shorter-range sea-based systems and unconventional delivery means should not be dismissed. The intelligence community considers that North Korea's Taepo Dong-2 missile, testing of which could occur at any time, has the throwweight to deliver a nuclear weapon to the United States. Iran probably, and Iraq possibly, will achieve a similar capability within the next fifteen years. Iran, Iraq, and other nations could shorten their development times by purchasing existing intercontinental ballistic missiles or space launch vehicles, which would bypass lengthy indigenous development programs and result in an intercontinental ballistic missile capability with little warning. Libya would appear to need to rely on this route to achieve this capability in the foreseeable future. In short, although there is substantial uncertainty with regard to the timing and the details of this emerging ballistic missile threat to the United States, there is virtual certainty that it is on the way.[13]

Why are rogue nations pursuing weapons of mass destruction and intercontinental ballistic missile delivery systems? It's important to recognize that the primary motivation is not to attack the United States in the midst of a crisis or conflict. Such an attack would almost certainly have extremely severe if not devastating consequences for the attacker. Rather than for purposes of warfighting or revenge, rogue nations view intercontinental ballistic missiles as "strategic weapons of deterrence and coercive diplomacy."[14] If the United States becomes vulnerable to direct attack by weapons of mass destruction, rogue nations believe, probably correctly, that U.S. freedom of action in regions of interest to them will be impaired. In a replay of the Persian Gulf War with Iraq armed with nuclear weapons on intercontinental ballistic missiles, we might well have chosen an alternative course of action rather than invading Iraq. And U.S. implicit threats to retaliate with nuclear weapons for chemical or biological attacks by Iraq might not have been effective.

The fundamental problem posed by rogue nations as they acquire weapons of mass destruction and delivery systems is that we're unsure of the efficacy of a strategy of deterrence when directed at these nations. If we don't fully understand their priorities or their logic, or if they believe they have little to lose, or if the U.S. retaliatory threat has not been clearly conveyed or is otherwise not completely credible, or if we are not able to identify the origin of the attack, deterrence of use of weapons of mass destruction by rogue nations could fail. The U.S. deterrent is further undermined when the U.S. threat of retaliation is asymmetric (i.e., nuclear response to chemical or biological attacks, since we have forsworn chemical and biological weapons), thus viewed as an escalation, thus not a reasonable response, and thus unlikely.

U.S. national security strategy with respect to the use of weapons of mass destruction by rogue nations is intentionally ambiguous. We do not threaten automatic nuclear retaliation; rather we *reserve the right* to respond to such attacks by nuclear retaliation. Since U.S. declaratory policy also includes possible first use of nuclear weapons, preemption of (presumably) imminent attack by rogue nations is also an option. It is likely that U.S. actual response will be determined by considering multiple factors: the level and likelihood of the threat, the expected immediate efficacy of the response, the anticipated effectiveness of any defenses we might have, and the perceived long-term consequences for U.S. national interests. In contrast to the case of a massive Russian attack, the United States will surely survive a rogue nation attack by weapons of mass destruction and have to live in the world that is shaped both by this attack and the U.S. response. Thus, in addition to the implications of nuclear retaliation for proliferation of nuclear weapons and for lowering of the nuclear threshold, we must also consider the implications for the continued efficacy of deterrence.

For purposes of this analysis, there are several additional points to be made about the threat posed by rogue nations. First, it is not at all certain that a strategy of deterrence will not be successful. In fact, the available evidence suggests the opposite. Deterrence by threat of nuclear retaliation to Iraqi biological and chemical attacks in the Persian Gulf War apparently was successful. It is also worth noting that deterrence of both Russia and China during the Cold War was also viewed as problematic. U.S. views of those nations, especially when they first acquired nuclear weapons, was not dissimilar to U.S. views of rogue nations today.

Second, the U.S. implied threat of nuclear retaliation to deter chemical and biological as opposed to nuclear attacks, which could become explicit in a crisis, could backfire. The more effective the threat is perceived to be, the more desirable nuclear weapons will be to rogue nations. Alternatively, if the nuclear retaliatory threat is ignored or not believed and a chemical or biological attack does take place, the United States may choose nonetheless not to execute the threat. This could undermine the credibility of such a threat in the next crisis, no matter how much damage we inflict with conventional weaponry. Perversely, concern with this effect could drive us to respond with nuclear weapons when we otherwise would not.

To sum up to this point, the threat from rogue nations is both upon us and proliferating. We should not presume that strategic forces and doctrines designed against the Soviet/Russian threat are adequate against the rogue nation threat. But U.S. near obsession with the rogue nation threat and concomitant diminution of the Russian threat is not justified by an objective examination of the situation. Certainly, the Russian threat is and will indefinitely remain orders of magnitude greater than any rogue nation threat in terms of its potential consequences. And while some are comforted by the argument that Russia has no intent to attack us, this analysis has argued that we should not rely on such a fragile assessment. There would be no issue here—we could simply address both threats—except that U.S. primary response to the rogue nation threat focuses on national missile defenses, which will almost certainly exacerbate the Russian threat.

Renewed Emphasis on Ballistic Missile Defenses

Ballistic missile defenses were introduced for the first time in combat during the Persian Gulf War. Scud missiles launched by Iraq at Israel and Saudi Arabia were engaged by the U.S. Patriot theater ballistic missile defense system. At the time of the war, Patriot was believed to be militarily highly effective. Politically, it undoubtedly played a critical role in keeping Israel from retaliating against Iraq. In the aftermath of the war, however, a controversy arose about how effective Patriot really was in shooting down Scuds. Assessments vary, but it now appears that Patriot was not as effective as it initially appeared to be. The problem was that several unanticipated events occurred during the Scud flight. Scud fuel tanks broke up in mid-trajectory, creating a large number of objects for Patriot to sort out, and the Scud warheads exhibited spiral reentry trajectories that made intercept very difficult.

This Persian Gulf War experience gave impetus to missile defense programs in the United States. In addition to a plethora of theater missile defense programs, the United States has a research and development program underway for a national missile defense (NMD) system intended to counter the threat of intercontinental ballistic missile attack on any part of the United States by rogue nations. At the same time, the defense is not intended to have a major impact on Russian strategic forces, although part of the mission is to defeat small unauthorized or accidental launches from Russia as well.

The Commission to Assess the Ballistic Missile Threat to the United States (Rumsfeld Commission) has further motivated a sense of urgency in deploying national missile defenses and the need to plan for a more robust defense than might initially be deployed.[15] However, it is worth noting that the Rumsfeld Commission report does not endorse national missile defenses. It simply describes the growing ballistic missile threat to the United States and the eroding ability of the intelligence community to predict that threat. This point is reinforced by the comments of one of the Rumsfeld Commission members, Richard Garwin:[16]

Insofar as the Rumsfeld report is concerned, it should—and must—be regarded as neutral regarding missile defenses. The commissioners simply did not consider whether deploying the national ballistic missile system as currently conceived represented wisdom or folly. . . . If the Rumsfeld commission spent another six months looking at the capability of the proposed national missile defense system against the threats that we have identified, I believe that we would come to a similarly uniform conclusion—that it would not be technically effective.

If national missile defenses are charged with saving us from the rogue nation ballistic missile threat, just how well can we expect them to work? The short answer is that we simply just don't know. The NMD program is widely recognized as a high-risk program laboring under a compressed timetable. There is no guarantee of success. Many in the community believe that there is very little chance that the NMD program will be successful, partly because of the inherent technical difficulty of hit-to-kill interception, but mostly because of the ease of designing effective countermeasures. Others have faith that U.S. technological genius is up to the task. It is unlikely that we will ever resolve the issue of national missile defense effectiveness until these defenses are called upon in battle. Unfortunately, as the Patriot experience in the Persian Gulf War demonstrates, unpleasant surprises may be in store.

Uncertainty in national missile defense effectiveness has important ramifications.[17] Failure to recognize this uncertainty in the context of a crisis involving a rogue nation could result in a more aggressive U.S. posture than prudence might otherwise dictate. On the other hand, acknowledging even a remote possibility that defenses might not work perfectly could prove paralyzing, just as Kennedy did not strike Cuban missile sites because he wasn't completely confident in the complete success of such strikes. Russia is likely to judge interceptors as more capable than they really are, perhaps to the point of assuming that each interceptor will result in one reentry vehicle kill. This is a major reason Russia may come to a different judgment than we do on the effect of U.S. national missile defense on their strategic forces. On the positive side, rogue nations may make a similar judgment, which could contribute to their reluctance to use or threaten to use ballistic missiles against the United States.

It is interesting to consider that there is a technical solution to the problems of both low missile defense effectiveness and uncertainty. If national missile defenses are as vital as some would argue and it turns out that the current hit-to-kill approach does not prove workable, logic dictates that we ought to at least consider nuclear-armed interceptors. The conventional wisdom is, of course, that anything nuclear is taboo; ballistic missile defenses are no exception. And there will be difficult political and operational issues to address. One approach might be to deploy nuclear interceptors first and gradually phase in hit-to-kill interceptors as that technology proves successful. But if the judgment is made that effective nuclear defenses are worse than ineffective hit-to-kill defenses, one must question how vital national missile defenses really are. In any event, future seminal events (e.g., a nuclear weapon used in war anywhere in the world, or a ballistic missile with any type of warhead impacting on the United States) could motivate us to reassess the conventional wisdom.

After technology issues, the greatest obstacle to deploying national missile defenses is Russia's adamance with respect to the importance of the ABM Treaty. U.S. declarations to the contrary notwithstanding, Russia is extremely concerned with the adverse impact of U.S. defenses on Russia's dwindling strategic forces. The scenario most worrisome to Russia is, of course, that in which it is the United States that strikes first. This scenario turns even more nightmarish if Russia has not generated its forces and fails to launch its alert forces on tactical warning. Even if Russia can maintain a deployed force of 2,500 warheads under START III, its only survivable warheads will be those few on submarines on patrol at sea and on mobile ICBMs dispersed in the field. Assuming survivable alert rates of about 10 percent for these forces, on a day-to-day basis fewer than some 200 Russian warheads would probably survive a well-executed U.S. first strike. Since almost all concepts for U.S. national missile defenses call for at least this many interceptors, each and every surviving, retaliating Russian warhead could theoretically be engaged by the defense. Russian worst-case planning could well lead them to believe that only a random few might get through.

Russian worries are our worries. Our problem is not that we won't be hammered by a Russian retaliation. It is, rather, that the steps Russia is likely to take to resolve its problem with the possibility of an inadequate deterrent are destabilizing. As the analysis of the post–Cold War nuclear experience will highlight, Russia's reaction is likely to place even greater reliance on early generation of strategic forces in a crisis and a strategy of launch on tactical warning, as well as pre-emptive strike should an attack appear imminent.

As an aside, the logical fallacies of mirror imaging and linear projection introduced in the discussion of the diminution of the Russian threat are also well illustrated in the debate on national missile defenses. The argument has been made that since the United States is having difficulty developing nonnuclear hit-to-kill defense technology, there is little possibility that Russia, less technologically sophisticated, will be able to engage in a defensive arms race. It's a short step to conclude that even if Russia does deploy defenses, they won't work very well so we don't have to worry about them. What this argument fails to recognize, however, is that Russia need not utilize the same hit-to-kill technology that the United States is developing. Any expansion of the Moscow ABM system will almost certainly also employ nuclear-armed defense interceptors. And those nuclear-armed interceptors are likely to work much better than U.S. hit-to-kill interceptors.

Moreover, since Russia's economy is a veritable basket case, and has been for some time, a linear projection of this state of affairs would support the argument that Russia can't possibly compete in an offense–defense arms race that U.S. deployment of defenses might otherwise spawn. While this may be true now and even for the near-term future, this argument implicitly assumes that Russia will continue to be unable to compete indefinitely. This is highly improbable; the Russian economy will recover someday, almost certainly sooner than a linear extrapolation of current trends would indicate.

THE POST–COLD WAR NUCLEAR EXPERIENCE

Nuclear theory—including deterrence theory, stability theory, and warfighting theory—is (fortunately) built on a meager foundation of hard data. Nuclear weapons have only been used in anger some four-and-one-half decades ago in a international environment far different from today's. And, of course, it is impossible to be certain that deterrence and stability theories are operating as expected. We can only be certain of their failures. So, how do we know we haven't constructed elaborate theoretical constructs in our minds that have little grounding in reality and will lead us astray in the next crisis? The answer is that we don't know, but we have to do the best we can. This philosophy should motivate us to take every opportunity to glean insights from the surprisingly large number of events that have occurred, especially since the end of the Cold War, in which nuclear weapons played a significant role, albeit short of actual use. These events have occurred at the alarming rate of nearly one per year:

- During the 1990–1991 Persian Gulf War, the United States implicitly, and apparently successfully, threatened Saddam Hussein with a nuclear response if Iraq used chemical or biological weapons.

- During the August 1991 coup attempt against Gorbachev, coup leaders placed the Soviet Union's strategic nuclear forces on a heightened state of alert.

- Under the guise of a military exercise, Russia again alerted its strategic nuclear forces during the October 1993 Russian parliamentary crisis.

- The United States confronted North Korea in 1994 over its extraction of weapons-grade plutonium from reactors.

- In January 1995 a multistage sounding rocket launched from Norway caused Russia to believe it might be under attack.

- China attempted to influence Taiwanese elections by launching ballistic missiles to waters off Taiwan in March 1996, and made implicit nuclear threats against the United States.

- In 1998 India announced its nuclear capability to the world by conducting a series of nuclear tests, and Pakistan quickly followed suit.

Lengthy as this list might appear, any such listing can only fail to convey the role that nuclear weapons play in avoiding such events in the first place. The simple possession of nuclear weapons by particular states has an unheralded daily effect on international relations in general and major military actions in particular. They are an important part of the landscape on which the game of geopolitics is played. They define implicit rules, limits, and dangers. North Korea has not attacked South Korea. China has not attacked Taiwan. Japan has not seized the Northern Territories from Russia. Israel has not been attacked by its Arab neighbors since it has been credited with acquiring nuclear weapons. Taiwan has not declared independence from China. The list of events that have not happened is literally endless. The claim is not that nuclear weapons were completely responsible for all these nonevents, only that nuclear weapons had an influence on the nonoccurrence of an important subset of them. Alliance relationships and the makeup of the U.N. Security Council are also clearly affected, if not driven, by nuclear weapon status. And nations under the U.S. nuclear umbrella are not coerced or intimidated as they otherwise would be.

Another important reason to examine these historical events is to stimulate U.S. thinking about a scenario-based calculus. If we can identify multiple plausible (or at least not implausible) paths to nuclear conflict that, as a set, could supplement the massive Russian attack scenario of the Cold War, we will have established the foundation for a post–Cold War strategic calculus.

Limited space does not permit an exhaustive recounting of all these nuclear-related events. The ones involving Russia are most relevant to this analysis, and among those the 1991 coup attempt against Gorbachev and the 1995 Norwegian meteorological rocket launch provide particularly instructive examples of how we might proceed to construct a post–Cold War strategic calculus.[18]

The 1991 Coup Attempt Against Gorbachev

The first post–Cold War nuclear experience occurred during the failed coup attempt against Soviet President Mikhail Gorbachev that began on August 18, 1991. The coup was led by Vladimir Kryuchkov, chairman of the KGB, with the active collaboration of the chief of the General Staff, the minister of Defense, the minister of Internal Affairs, the prime minister, the deputy chairman of the Defense Council, the vice president, and others—in short, the most powerful men in the Soviet government other than Gorbachev himself.

The geopolitical situation had been changing dramatically for the worse for the Soviet Union over the past several years. The Warsaw Treaty Organization had collapsed. The Red Army had pulled out of Eastern Europe, which promptly overthrew communist rule and established new democracies. Germany was unifying. And the United States had just convincingly demonstrated its conventional military prowess in the Persian Gulf War against a former ally of the Soviet Union. Gorbachev's policies were blamed for these events, which, prior to Gorbachev, would have universally been viewed as catastrophes in the Soviet Union. The straw that broke the camel's back was Gorbachev's plan for a vote on a Union Treaty to establish a new constitution for the Soviet Union. Gorbachev's objective was to establish the legitimacy of Soviet rule, but the coup plotters adamantly believed that the inevitable defeat of the Union Treaty would lead to the disintegration of the Soviet Union.

During the afternoon of August 18, two days before the scheduled vote on the Union Treaty, the State Committee for the State of Emergency sent a delegation to Gorbachev at his Black Sea resort at Foros. After failing to persuade Gorbachev to accept a change of leadership, they severed his communication links with the outside world and held him under house arrest. The delegation also seized Gorbachev's "nuclear briefcase," a portable display and communications device with which nuclear strikes could be ordered. Since the other two such devices were held by the minister of Defense and the chief of the General Staff, this act gave the coup plotters control of all three such devices. By the positions they held in the Soviet military and civilian leadership and their seizures of the nuclear briefcases, the coup leaders, and no one else, clearly controlled the Soviet Union's strategic forces. During the night they ordered their military forces, including the strategic nuclear forces, to be placed on Increased Combat Readiness, analogous to the United States going to a state of generated alert. Early the next morning, August 19, at 6:00 A.M., they announced the coup to the world.

The question of most importance for this analysis is this: Why did the coup leaders alert the strategic nuclear forces of the Soviet Union? Perhaps it was to demonstrate authority and control in order to enhance the prospects for the coup's success. Alternatively, it might have been intended as a means of establishing internal order and discipline, although this makes sense only if the worry was that unauthorized Russian launches might take place, which, in turn, doesn't make any sense at all. However, the explanation that rings most true is that the coup leaders genuinely feared the possibility of U.S. exploitation of a potentially chaotic situation. Alerting their strategic forces prepared the Soviet Union to respond to a U.S. attack. If we can once again suppress the tendency to mirror image and consider the unreconstructed Cold War attitudes of the coup leaders with respect to the threat of a U.S. surprise attack, it is highly likely that they truly believed that the United States might actually attack during the coup in spite of the fact that, to most Americans, even contemplating such an action borders on the incredible. This interpretation is also supported by direct statements from coup leaders and service commanders in the aftermath.

One seemingly anomalous event occurred during the move to Increased Combat Readiness: mobile SS25 intercontinental ballistic missiles that had been dispersed in the field returned to garrison. When the United States generates its strategic forces, it makes them both ready to launch and less vulnerable—submarines are put to sea and bombers are placed on strip or airborne alert. So, why would the coup leaders make Soviet SS25s more vulnerable by returning them to garrison, especially if they were concerned about the possibility of a U.S. attack? Alternative explanations also exist for this. At the time it was widely interpreted in the United States as a signal by the coup leaders that the move to Increased Combat Readiness was not hostile, but rather a defensive act. However, with the Soviet Union at Increased Combat Readiness there was high probability that these missiles would survive even in garrison by launching on tactical warning or preemptively striking the United States as it prepared to attack. So the return of SS25s to garrison probably did not greatly increase their vulnerability, but it did increase the coup leaders' control over possible disobedience by launch crews if the need came to issue a launch order.

It is ironic that U.S. misinterpretation of the coup leaders' intentions in returning SS25s to garrison may have served to dampen the crisis. During the coup the United States very carefully took no military actions to fuel the fears of the coup leaders. If the United States had tried to meddle in some overt way, or alerted its strategic forces in response to the Soviet move to Increased Combat Readiness, or was in the midst of a large-scale military exercise, there is just no telling how events might have unfolded.

The coup failed when military officers refused to storm the Soviet Parliament building, the so-called White House, at which anticoup demonstrators led by Boris Yeltsin were protesting. The coup leaders planned to retake the building in a military operation to be conducted the night of August 20, but key officers refused to participate. Coup leaders, some of whom were drunk on the last day of the coup, were arrested. Several committed suicide, others stood trial and were imprisoned. It was all over by August 21, and Soviet nuclear forces stood down from alert.

The 1995 Norwegian Meteorological Rocket Launch

Probably the best-known and certainly the shortest-duration post–Cold War nuclear event occurred on the morning of January 25, 1995. At 6:24 A.M., Greenwich Mean Time, Norwegian and American scientists launched a scientific sounding rocket from the Andoya Island range on the Norwegian Sea to investigate the aurora borealis. Although hundreds of launches had been conducted from Andoya over a period spanning several decades of the Cold War and post–Cold War eras, this launch was the first involving a multistage rocket. Following established practices, Norway had notified the Russian embassy in Oslo that a launch was planned, the type of rocket, and the intended impact point, and provided a rather imprecise launch window (January 15–February 5, between 5 A.M. and noon). Greater precision was deemed impractical because the actual launch time depended on unpredictable weather.

Unfortunately, in a bureaucratic snafu the details of which are still not entirely clear, this information was never passed to the Russian military, in particular to the military officers manning Russia's Missile Attack Warning System. Their first notification appeared on their radar screens. They quickly identified the missile as a threat, dutifully passed a warning up the chain of command to the General Staff, which then relayed the report to the nuclear briefcases held by the president, the Defense minister, and the chief of the General Staff. A telephone conference call among them was arranged. All this occurred within a matter of a few minutes as the missile was still ascending.

Presumably if they were certain they were under attack they would have immediately ordered a counterattack. The situation must have appeared ambiguous. On one hand, there was no ongoing crisis that might portend an attack. And only one missile appeared to be involved. However, the error associated with launch-point estimation was consistent with a launch from a submarine in the Norwegian sea, and the multistage rocket was consistent with a multistage sea-launched ballistic missile. Moreover, a single missile could suggest an electromagnetic pulse attack, a high-altitude burst that could disable Russia's early warning system and command, control, and communications of their strategic forces as a precursor to a major attack.

As they considered their options, including destroying the missile with the antiballistic missile system deployed around Moscow and launching Russia's strategic forces, the sounding rocket's trajectory eventually veered off to the northeast, away from Russia. The crisis ended when the rocket impacted twenty-four minutes after launch.

TOWARD A POST–COLD WAR
STRATEGIC CALCULUS

What lessons can we draw from this analysis of the post–Cold War strategic environment and nuclear experience? First, it is true, and obvious as well, that in spite of the large number of nuclear-related events in the post–Cold War era, they all ended without a nuclear strike. Some might argue that this is evidence of the robustness of deterrence and stability as currently understood and practiced. After all, the more allegedly close calls, the less close they seem. But a more probing examination of the coup attempt against Gorbachev and the Norwegian meteorological rocket launch, as well as the other nuclear-related events, coupled with a little bit of imagination on how things might have come out differently given a slight change of circumstances, results in quite the opposite assessment: We have been lucky, and there's no telling when our luck might run out.

A second general lesson we can draw is that we should expect to be surprised by the details of future nuclear events. We can't anticipate every scenario that might lead to nuclear war, and we have no real way to judge their likelihoods. Nuclear conflict could arise from internal upheavals, erroneous tactical warning (including misinterpreted exercises/wargames, test/training launches, or a U.S. national missile defense launch), accidental launches, unauthorized launches, preemption of or response to use of chemical or biological weapons, Russian invasion of the Baltic States as they attempt to join NATO, third nation attacks on the United States or Russia, third-nation regional conflicts (e.g., India and Pakistan), conventional military operations on the periphery of Russia, and any number of other scenarios.

Third, we should not count on getting strategic warning. We need a strategic warning paradigm broader than we had during the Cold War, when we expected that any conflict over Europe that might end with a massive nuclear exchange would be preceded by a lengthy crisis with plenty of time to generate U.S. strategic forces. Russia's internal problems, of which we may be blithely unaware, can now be a source of nuclear danger. It is important to recognize that both the coup attempt against Gorbachev and the Norwegian meteorological rocket launch were essentially one-sided crises. Not only might we not get strategic warning, but if we do get strategic warning we must carefully weigh the possible impact of our response on Russian perceptions. Alerting U.S. strategic forces in the midst of either of these scenarios would have been extremely destabilizing.

Finally, mirror imaging is not the only dangerous mode of thinking. The U.S. lack of awareness and/or indifference to Russian perspectives is also a serious problem. In particular, we have difficulty fully appreciating the extent of Russian paranoia. Russian paranoia is often attributed to Russia's brutal historical experiences, particularly during World War II, but it also probably reflects a degree of—once again— mirror imaging, this time on their part. Since the Soviet Union had global hegemonic ambitions, the Soviet Union believed—and now Russia believes—the same of us. Since Russia's nuclear strategy calls for preemptive attack when war appears imminent, they believe we are also ready to strike at a moment's notice. And on and on it goes.

Are Nuclear Weapons Still Relevant?

This is not an entirely trivial question. It is asked here because the Canberra Commission and others have argued that now that the Cold War is over the only reason nuclear weapons are needed is because other states possess them.[19] So in theory we ought to be able to find a way to simultaneously eliminate both the worldwide possession of nuclear weapons and the need of individual states to possess them. Unfortunately, neither the post–Cold War strategic environment nor the post–Cold War experience with nuclear-related events supports this hypothesis.

Clearly, nuclear weapons remain relevant to all states that possess them and all states that are attempting to acquire them. They are also relevant to all states allied with or otherwise under the nuclear umbrella of nuclear weapons states, and are relevant in less tangible ways to other nations. In fact, the worrisome trend is that nuclear weapons are becoming increasingly relevant to a greater number of states. And the relevance of nuclear weapons is not just to counter other states' nuclear weapons. States also clearly acquire nuclear weapons to counter conventional threats. Israel provides probably the clearest example of this motivation. As biological and chemical weapons proliferate, nuclear weapons will undoubtedly be perceived as increasingly necessary to counter these threats as well. So if nuclear weapons are to become irrelevant, so too must large-scale conventional combat and other weapons of mass destruction.

What has become less important in the post–Cold War era is U.S. reliance on first use of nuclear weapons, even though the United States still maintains a declaratory policy that includes the option for first use. U.S. conventional superiority, especially in Europe but also around the world, has reduced the need to threaten first use of nuclear weapons, especially against Russia. The unfortunate side effect of this great imbalance in conventional power is that potentially hostile states increasingly perceive the need to acquire nuclear weapons and to pose asymmetric threats, especially involving other weapons of mass destruction.

Perhaps the reason the relevance of nuclear weapons is questioned is that we *wish* they were no longer relevant because of their inherent dangers and U.S. conventional superiority. Unfortunately, wishing won't make it so.

Is Nuclear Deterrence Still a Relevant Strategy, and How Should We Assess the Contribution of Strategic Forces to Underwriting It?

Nuclear deterrence is clearly the strategy of choice for avoiding both nuclear and nonnuclear wars in the post–Cold War era. Both Russia and the United States rely on nuclear deterrence. So do China, Israel, India, Pakistan, and, to a lesser extent, the United Kingdom and France. While the United States no longer faces a conventional threat that could require a nuclear response, it has now invoked nuclear deterrence to deal with emerging biological and chemical threats. Similarly, Russia now invokes nuclear deterrence to deal with hitherto nonexistent conventional threats. Rogue states anticipate that acquisition of nuclear weapons will enable them to deter U.S. intervention in regional crises. The situation is crystal clear: Nuclear deterrence is relied upon when other options do not exist or are impractical. This was true during the Cold War and remains true today.

That nuclear deterrence is thriving does not mean that nuclear warfighting is not. All nations with nuclear weapons devise plans for their use should deterrence fail. And as more and more nations acquire nuclear weapons, there are more and more opportunities for deterrence to fail. Then we're likely to find out what all those warfighting doctrines are. Also, as the strategic arsenals of at least the United States and Russia are reduced there may be more opportunities for successful preemptive strikes. India and Pakistan, with nascent arsenals, may be especially vulnerable to such attacks from each other.

A more interesting question is how much further the United States can safely reduce its strategic arsenal (under START III, for example) without adversely affecting its deterrence strategy. Answering this using the Cold War strategic calculus would require delving into the details of targeting and its associated measure of effectiveness, damage expectancy. This would require a lengthier discussion than can be provided here. Suffice it to say that the Cold War approach of establishing a requirement to hold at risk a certain set of targets is very much a judgment call, more art than science, and this judgment has varied immensely over the course of the Cold War and post–Cold War eras. Establishing targeting goals and then treating them as if they were sacrosanct may no longer serve U.S. purposes. Furthermore, when a national leader is contemplating the decision of whether or not to go to nuclear war, the detailed calculus of damage expectancy is probably far down the list of his considerations. The things that damage expectancy ignores—casualties, environmental damage, and societal damage—probably weigh much more heavily.

One way out of the Cold War targeting/damage-expectancy analytical morass is to concentrate on the more straightforward measure of arriving weapons in the U.S. post–Cold War strategic calculus. If Russia attacks the United States, or vice versa, how many retaliatory weapons can the attacker expect to detonate on his own country? The answer to that question cuts to the heart of the effectiveness of deterrence. To determine how far a nation can safely reduce (by arms control) its arsenal, it must answer this question for the worst plausible scenario: when that country is on the receiving end of a first strike and is on day-to-day alert and cannot, or does not, launch on tactical warning. Figure 3.1 presents this measure of deterrence, *assured retaliation,* for both the United States and the Soviet Union/Russia at the beginning of the post–Cold War era and under three successive START regimes.

Figure 3.1
Assured Retaliation

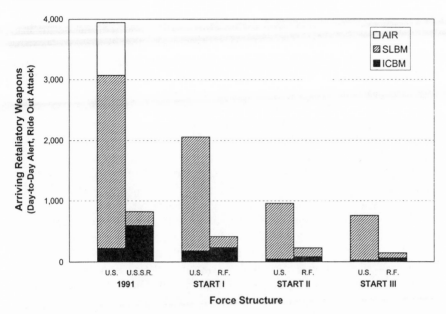

The ordinate of Figure 3.1 shows number of warheads of the retaliator (second striker) that survive a first strike, are reliable, and penetrate the defenses of the first striker. For example, if Russia struck first in 1991, the United States in the day-to-day alert, ride-out-attack scenario could have retaliated with nearly 4,000 reliable arriving warheads from all three legs of the strategic triad. This assured retaliation declines steadily for the United States with each new START treaty to about 750 under a hypothetical START III treaty, and is now composed of weapons almost entirely from the submarine leg of the triad. Whether this U.S. assured retaliation is adequate for deterrence of Russian attack is left to the reader to judge, although the ultimate decision rests with the Russian civilian and military leadership.

The Russian assured retaliation has consistently been significantly less that the U.S. assured retaliation, which could indicate Russia's intention to avoid this scenario (day-to-day alert, ride-out attack), and explains their doctrinal preference for preemptive attack. Of utmost significance is the drop in Russia's assured retaliation to fewer than 200 weapons under START III. While we may perceive this as an adequate deterrent, Russia assuredly does not. Russia's inadequate assured retaliation is the source of Russia's concern about U.S. national missile defenses and the underlying source of first-strike instability.

Is First-Strike Stability Still a Relevant Concept, and How Should We Evaluate It?

In the United States, first-strike stability was conceived as an important element of the Cold War strategic calculus that would apply in the context of a bilateral crisis, such as the Cuban missile crisis, in which there is some expectation of nuclear war. It purports to capture the contribution that force structure and posture make to each side's decision of whether to strike first or wait. There have been no such crises in the post–Cold War era. The closest we came was the Norwegian rocket launch incident, but that was a one-sided crisis and for Russia the issue was not strike first or wait, but launch on tactical warning or wait. On the other hand, perhaps we should not be too surprised that no such crises have occurred during the post–Cold War era. Few such crises occurred during the Cold War.

From a Western perspective, the answer to the question strike first or wait will invariably be to wait. Unless evidence for an impending attack is completely overwhelming, the only answer that will result in an acceptable outcome is to wait. Striking first just guarantees a catastrophic result. Russia's perspective is different. They view the wait option as much riskier because of the low level of their assured retaliation. So they would feel correspondingly greater pressure to strike first.

While the Cold War conception of first-strike stability may or may not remain relevant, there are two other aspects of stability that seem especially important in the post–Cold War era and should be part of any post–Cold War strategic calculus: *generation stability* and *prompt launch stability*. In the coup attempt against Gorbachev, one of the first steps taken was to place Russia's military forces, including its strategic nuclear forces, on Increased Combat Readiness. Generating strategic forces is fraught with possibilities for misunderstanding and crisis escalation, and thus potentially destabilizing. The decision to generate is affected by the structure and day-to-day posture of strategic forces, and hence amenable to quantitative analysis. Figure 3.2 presents such an analysis, again for both sides at the beginning of the post–Cold War era and under successive START regimes.

The ordinate of Figure 3.2 is the benefit derived from force generation, measured as the percentage increase in the arriving retaliatory weapons of the second striker. For example, in 1991 if the United States launches its retaliation on warning (refer to leftmost black bar), it would increase the number of arriving retaliatory weapons by about 60 percent by generating its forces, compared to the case in which the United States also launches its retaliation on warning but remains on day-to-day alert. If the United States rides out the attack instead, the increase in U.S. reliable arriving retaliatory warheads is approximately 90 percent. The important message of Figure 3.2 is the extremely large Rus-

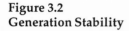

Figure 3.2
Generation Stability

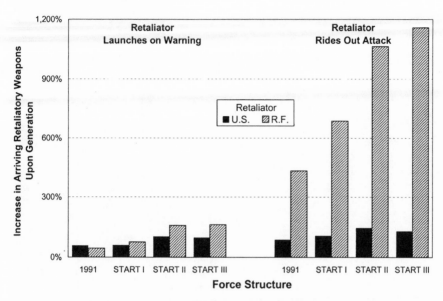

sian sensitivity to force generation when Russia rides out the attack. This sensitivity is over 400 percent in 1991 and increases with each successive START treaty to nearly 1,200 percent under START III. In other words, under a prospective START III treaty Russia can increase its retaliation on the United States by twelve times if it generates its forces before the United States can attack. This is a reflection of the vulnerability of Russian strategic forces on day-to-day alert and explains Russia's propensity for early generation, as occurred during the coup attempt against Gorbachev.

The second aspect of stability not directly addressed by first-strike stability relates to the decision of whether or not to launch on tactical warning. This was clearly the issue faced by Russia during the Norwegian rocket launch. Although a decision in that crisis was ultimately not necessary, it is not too difficult to imagine circumstances in which such a decision is forced. Thus, it is worth trying to configure strategic force structure and posture to encourage a decision to not launch on tactical warning, but rather to wait until incontrovertible information about the reality and scope of an attack is available. Figure 3.3 presents an analysis of the sensitivity of both the United States and Russia to launch on tactical warning.

Figure 3.3 is analogous to Figure 3.2, except that now the ordinate measures the benefit to launching on warning compared to riding out a first strike. The ordinate of Figure 3.3 is the percentage increase in

Figure 3.3
Prompt Launch Stability

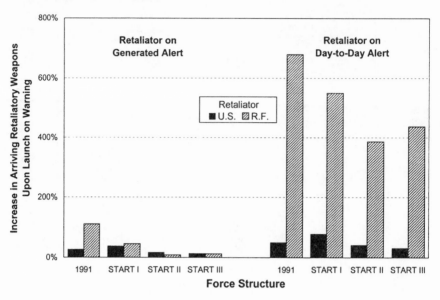

the arriving retaliatory weapons of the retaliator if he launches on warning, compared to the case in which he rides out the attack. The two scenarios, corresponding to the left and right halves of Figure 3.3, are when the retaliator is on generated alert and when the retaliator is on day-to-day alert. Again, we see an extremely large Russian sensitivity to launch on tactical warning caused by Russia's low assured retaliation. The START I and START II treaties reduce this sensitivity to launch on tactical warning somewhat, but START III reverses this trend. Under START III, if Russia retaliates from a day-to-day alert posture, Russia's increase in the number of warheads in its retaliation increases by over 400 percent. This high sensitivity indicates the pressure Russia feels in crises such as the Norwegian rocket launch.

It is interesting that the driver of first-strike instability is the existence of vulnerable forces. If a country has no vulnerable forces, it can inflict the same level of damage on another country whether it strikes first or second. The two sources of vulnerable forces are those that are not on alert (e.g., all U.S. and some Russian submarines in port and both sides' bombers) and those that are on alert but are targetable (e.g., ICBMs in silos and some Russian submarines in port). Some forces in the not-on-alert category are made invulnerable by placing them on alert (e.g., putting submarines to sea). Those that remain vulnerable (e.g., bombers on strip alert) and those in the alert-but-targetable category need to rely on prompt launch to survive. So sensitivity to generation and sensitivity to prompt launch capture the essential elements of first-strike stability. It is not clear that a separate measure of first-strike stability is needed or useful.

NEXT STEPS

This analysis has only dabbled with the preliminary steps toward a strategic calculus for the post–Cold War era. Much additional thought, work, and inspiration is needed. Most fundamentally, a more thorough analysis of the post–Cold War threat environment and nuclear experience is imperative. Then we have to bite the bullet and develop a set of scenarios, one by one, for which we can envision a role for nuclear weapons. These scenarios should be specific enough to clearly identify the roles of nuclear weapons and the application of nuclear strategy and to develop appropriate measures of strategic force effectiveness. Such a set might ultimately include a number of different scenarios involving each nuclear weapons state.

We might also take this opportunity to reexamine existing analytical practices and measures of effectiveness with an eye toward improving them: Damage expectancy and first-strike stability come foremost to mind. But we also need to be more sophisticated in nuclear war modeling for policy analysis. Rather than treating strategic nuclear weapons in isolation, we need to consider integrated analyses that also involve tactical nuclear weapons, biological and chemical weapons, and advanced conventional weapons. Rather than the simple first-strike/retaliation nuclear exchange, we need to consider multistage nuclear wars with evolving objectives. Rather than ignoring the issue of strategic weapons reserves, we need to recognize the increasing importance of them and to consider their utility in the postwar international situation. Finally, we need to develop methods to analyze ballistic missile defenses more realistically, especially by explicitly acknowledging uncertainties in defense effectiveness, and to extend bilateral stability constructs to a multilateral context.

As a closing thought, Russia appears to have a more clearly articulated nuclear doctrine that reflects post–Cold War realities than the United States. And, in the tradition of the Soviet Union, Russia has emphasized quantitative analysis of nuclear doctrine and arms control policy. If for no reason other than to gain important insights into Russian perspectives, we ought to try to understand their post–Cold War strategic calculus.

NOTES

The views expressed in this chapter are those of the author. They do not necessarily represent the views of the Department of State, the Defense Threat

Reduction Agency, or the U.S. government. The author wishes to thank Dr. Peter Vincent Pry, military advisor to the U.S. Congress and former CIA analyst, for many private conversations on the nature of the Russian threat, and for prepublication access to *War Scare: The United States and Russia on the Nuclear Brink* (Westport, Conn.: Praeger Publishers, 1999). Figures presented in this chapter are based on data found in Appendix B and assumptions discussed in Chapter 6.

1. Glenn A. Kent and David E. Thaler, *First-Strike Stability: A Methodology for Evaluating Strategic Forces*, R-3765-AF (Santa Monica, Calif.: RAND Corporation, 1989). Although the Kent/Thaler index of first-strike stability has achieved some degree of recognition in the defense analysis community, there are serious conceptual, mathematical, and practical problems with this measure.

2. *Military Doctrine of the Russian Federation*, reprinted in Moscow Krasnaya Zxvezda, 9 October 1999.

3. *Basic Provisions of the Military Doctrine of the Russian Federation*, translated in FBIS-SOV-93-222-5 (19 November 1993), p. 3.

4. Ibid.

5. Lieutenant General G. D. Ivanov, *Main Points of a Presentation by Russian Federation Assistant Minister of Defense for Military Policy*, October 1994.

6. Ibid., 4.

7. *Russian Federation National Security Blueprint*, 17 December 1977, translated in FBIS-SOV-97-364 (30 December 1997); and Richard R. Starr, "Russia's New Blueprint for National Security," *Strategic Review* 26, no. 2 (1998): 31–42.

8. Member of the Russian parliament and leader of the misnamed Liberal Democratic Party of Russia.

9. Former general of the 14th Army in Moldova, former secretary of the Russian Security Council, and former presidential candidate.

10. Russian author (*One Day in the Life of Ivan Denisovich, The Gulag Archipelago*, etc.), dissident, Nobel laureate, and former gulag prisoner.

11. Keith B. Payne, *Deterrence in the Second Nuclear Age* (Lexington: University Press of Kentucky, 1996).

12. U.S. Department of State Daily Press Briefing, 7 April 1994.

13. National Intelligence Council, *Foreign Missile Developments and the Ballistic Missile Threat to the United States Through 2015* (Washington, D.C.: Central Intelligence Agency, 1999).

14. Ibid., 1.

15. Donald Rumsfeld et al., *Report of the Commission to Assess the Ballistic Missile Threat to the United States*, 15 July 1998.

16. Richard L. Garwin, "The Rumsfeld Report: What We Did." *Bulletin of the Atomic Scientists* 54, no. 6 (1998): 40–41.

17. See J. Scouras et al., *The Defense Contribution to Uncertainty* (Rosslyn, Va.: System Planning Corporation, 1984), for a quantitative analysis of uncertainty in defense effectiveness.

18. See Peter V. Pry, *War Scare: Russia and America on the Nuclear Brink* (Westport, Conn.: Praeger, 1999), for detailed accounts of the 1991 coup attempt against Gorbachev and the 1995 Norwegian meteorological rocket launch, as well as other nuclear events not discussed here.

19. Richard Butler et al., *Report of the Canberra Commission on the Elimination of Nuclear Weapons* (Canberra: National Capital Printers, 1996).

4

Russian–American Nuclear Stability Issues: Opportunities and Risks in the Twenty-First Century

Frederic S. Nyland

The purpose of this chapter is to examine various aspects of arms reduction between the United States and Russia that may emerge in the twenty-first century. The focus of this chapter will be on the strategic nuclear forces of these two countries and some of the potential prospects as well as the problems that might be encountered. At present, arms reductions are being accomplished in accordance with the START I Treaty.[1] Even so, Russia and the United States still retain a very large number of strategic nuclear weapons. Agreement on the terms of the START II Treaty has been achieved.[2] The U.S. Senate and the Russian Duma have ratified START II. Negotiations for START III lie in the future.[3] In spite of the apparent satisfactory political relationships between the two nations, either the United States or Russia each retain more nuclear weapons than those of all other nations combined. With or without further reductions in strategic nuclear armaments, there is a need to consider the interactions of the world's two largest nuclear powers under present and future political and military conditions. In this chapter attention is devoted to future bipolar conditions as they may prevail beyond START II into the twenty-first century.

Strategic nuclear inventories of the United States and Russia are shown in Figure 4.1 along with some possible reductions in the strategic nuclear warheads of the two countries. The situation as of January 1999 is shown first. The inventories are 7,958 for the United States and 6,578 for Russia. The terms of the START II treaty would be met with the forces shown next.[4] The upper bound suggested for the warhead

Figure 4.1
Present and Potential Warhead Reductions

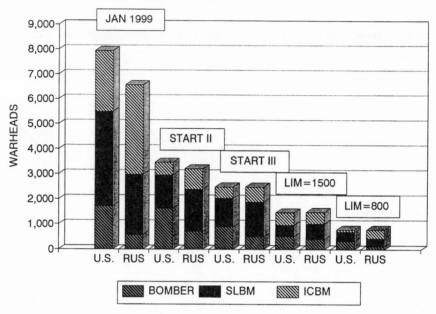

limits under the START III negotiations is 2,500. Beyond the potential terms of START III, some have suggested a lower limit of 1,500 warheads.[5] The lowest warhead limit shown in the figure is 800. In this chapter we will address some of the prospects and problems involved in two different levels of warheads, 2,500 and 800. A limit of 2,500 warheads (perhaps as low as 2,000) may be evolving and come to pass in the near future. Discussions about reductions to 1,000 warheads or less have been suggested elsewhere.[6] In this chapter we will also consider a lower limit of 800 warheads for each side. This limit should not be construed as an issue for which the author is a zealous advocate, but rather as an example of a much greater reduction than is now being publicly discussed.

Before embarking on examinations of prospects and problems, the next section of this chapter will present some assumptions, and will be followed by a brief description of the methods used to evaluate the issues addressed. Issues in later sections of this chapter will include first-strike stability and several factors that may result in its degradation within the two warhead limits considered here. Aspects of geopolitical stability may prevail to lower first-strike stability, and trade-offs between these two measures will be considered. There could be a substantial risk of unintentional nuclear exchanges if either or both sides were to implement the tactic of launching nuclear forces on tactical warning of attack. Such a tactic, while extremely dangerous, could evolve as a last resort, especially in a crisis situation. What happens if one side or the other decides to cheat or "break out" of treaty obligations by secretly increasing the number of warheads carried by existing strategic weapon systems? One section of this chapter will examine such activities and their potential consequences. Finally, a summary and our observations will be presented.

ASSUMPTIONS ABOUT FORCES, DEFENSES, AND TARGETS

The purpose of this section is to indicate critical assumptions concerning the strategic nuclear forces of Russia and the United States, their defenses, and the distribution of valued assets. The assumptions about strategic forces will be rather specific in nature, but the reader should be wary of these. The general nature of the assumptions may be realized in the future, but not in the same form as the weapon systems treated in this chapter. There have been pressures for the United States to build and deploy strategic defenses against ballistic missiles. We will indicate the nature of our assumptions regarding this issue. Part of the target system for any first or retaliatory strike would be the valued assets of the United States and Russia. Analyses of first-strike stability depend on the number and distribution of these targets.

Strategic Nuclear Forces

Assumptions about the structure and posture of the strategic nuclear forces of Russia and the United States form an integral part of the analyses in this chapter. Structure is an enumeration of the kinds of weapon systems, and their posture refers to their state of readiness and disposition. In anticipating events that might lead to further arms reductions in the twenty-first century, we will examine two distinct cases: the possibility of successful negotiation of a START III treaty (2,500 warheads on each side), and a further reduction of strategic warheads to an even lower limit of 800 on each side. The number and type of weapons shown in Table 4.1 are illustrative examples, not predictions of the future.

The START III assumptions are based on a number of sources. It has been assumed that U.S. forces would be reduced below the levels of the START II treaty (3,000 to 3,500 warheads). The assumptions indicated for the United States are based on potential reductions projected beyond those of official U.S. Department of Defense documents and

Table 4.1
Assumed Force Structures and Postures

System Name	Pk vs. Base	Number of Bases	Warheads per Base	Alert Rate
START III, Limit = 2500 Warheads				
RUSSIA				
ICBM(Silo)	0.6	244	1	1.00
RS-12(Mobile)	0.8	40	9	0
Typhoon	0.7	6	160	0.33
Delfin	0.7	7	64	0.29
TU-95	0.8	10	36.8	0
TU-160	0.8	2	60	0
UNITED STATES				
Minuteman	0.6	448	1	1.00
Trident	0.7	12	96	0.67
B-52	0.8	10	58	0
B-2	0.8	2	160	0
LIMIT = 800 WARHEADS				
RUSSIA				
RS-12(Mobile)	0.8	33	9	0.30
Delfin	0.7	6	64	0.50
TU-160	0.8	2	60	0
UNITED STATES				
Minuteman	0.6	48	1	1.00
Trident	0.7	9	48	0.67
B-2	0.8	4	80	0

on an independent analysis of further reductions below START II.[7] On the Russian side, the indicated force structure is based on projections from an earlier work by a Russian analyst who examined force structures under the START II treaty.[8] For both sides, the alert rates are those assumed by the author. Alert rates can be a contentious isssue containing uncertainties, particularly for the Russians. Later we shall vary the Russian alert rates in an effort to capture their debilitating effect on first-strike stability.

Future Russian forces under START III may have three distinct elements: land-based intercontinental ballistic missiles (ICBMs), sea-launched ballistic missiles (SLBMs) carried by submarines, and bombers. Table 4.1 indicates the potential degree of vulnerability of each system (the probability of severe damage to a base by a single attacking warhead, Pk), the number of bases, the number of warheads in each base, and the alert rate. For mobile ICBMs the alert rate corresponds to the fraction of warheads deployed away from their garrisons. For SLBMs the alert rate corresponds to the fraction of warheads deployed at sea. For bombers the alert rate is the fraction of bomber weapons that are ready to depart their bases should tactical warning of a sudden attack be provided. Basically, it is assumed that alert forces are invulnerable to a swift attack.

Table 4.1 does not indicate the number of warheads that each side might bring to a fully generated readiness condition to implement a first strike. For the limit of 2,500 warheads, it is assumed that Russia could generate 1,504 reentry vehicles and 296 bomber weapons in preparation for a first strike against the United States. It is assumed that the United States could generate 1,495 reentry vehicles and 544 bomber weapons for a first strike against Russia. At the lower limit of 800 warheads each for both sides, it is assumed that Russia could generate 522 reentry vehicles and 72 bomber weapons for a first strike. It is assumed that the United States could generate 427 reentry vehicles and 224 bomber weapons for a first strike. These estimates reflect a very high alert rate for both sides, and operationally this condition probably could only be sustained for a short time.

The assumptions regarding a much lower limit of 800 strategic nuclear warheads for each side are estimates by the author for both force structures and force postures. These estimates were based on an overall assumption that each side would try to preserve a triad of nuclear forces (i.e., each side would preserve force elements of land-based ICBMs, sea-based SLBMs, and bombers), but much fewer in number. In Russia it was assumed that they would rely on mobile ICBMs, fewer strategic submarines, and fewer bombers. For the United States it was assumed that they would retain a token force of ICBMs in silos, nine strategic submarines, and the newest bomber, the B-2.

Strategic Defenses

Both the United States and Russia may decide to deploy strategic defenses to counter ballistic missile reentry vehicles. In the analysis to follow, the number of interceptors that each side may choose to deploy will be equal, and will defend value targets. The probability that a single interceptor can negate a reentry vehicle is assumed to be 0.7.

Both the United States and Russia are assumed to have strategic defenses to counter bombers or the weapons that bombers may carry. In the analysis to follow, it is assumed that the effect of these defenses is represented by a single number, the probability of bomber warheads penetrating the defenses. For both sides the probability of penetration is assumed to be 0.8; that is, 20 percent of the bomber weapons will be attrited by air defenses.

Valued Assets

Valued assets of both sides are targets to be attacked. Valued assets are defined as those bases containing projection forces, bases for support of projection or nuclear forces, defense industries, other critical industries, and leadership facilities. For Russia it is assumed that about 95 percent of valued assets are contained in 2,500 aimpoints.[9] For the United States we estimate that 95 percent of such assets are contained in about 3,000 aimpoints. Not all of these assets are of equal value, and are assumed to be exponentially distributed.

All the assumptions enumerated so far are those necessary to support analyses of first-strike stability, potential loss of deterrence, launch on warning tactics, and potential efforts by one or both sides to cheat on future treaties. Other assumptions will be made and explained as they are needed to support details of emerging analyses.

METHODOLOGY

A number of analysis methods will be employed in this chapter. It is not our intent to dwell on the mathematical details, but to describe each approach in general terms. The interested reader may consult the various references indicated.

First-Strike Stability

First-strike stability is a more demanding measure of deterrence than examination of central deterrence. First-strike stability is a two-sided measure between two nuclear powers.[10] The analysis is based on a scenario from which the equations and mathematical manipulations are derived.

The scenario used as a basis for examining first-strike stability involves two participating nations, Russia and the United States. The method involves the sequential analysis of first strikes by both parties. The first striker generates strategic forces by bringing as many weapons as possible to a readiness state from which they can be massively employed. Some of the warheads are allocated so as to destroy the defender's strategic nuclear forces (counterforce), and the remainder are allocated against aimpoints containing "value" (countervalue). The trick for the first striker is to adjust the counterforce and countervalue warheads within the bounds of warheads available for the first strike so as to minimize his "cost." It is then assumed that the defender retaliates by aiming all of his surviving warheads against the "value" targets of the first striker. In this analysis, cost is a function of the damage suffered by one side and the damage not inflicted on the other side.

The index of first-strike stability is the product of two cost ratios. The first ratio is the cost to Russia of going first to the cost to Russia going second. The second ratio is the cost to the United States of going first to the cost to the United States going second. When the first-strike stability index is high (nearly 1.0), neither side is tempted to strike first and the situation is quite stable. When the first-strike stability is low, approaching zero, either one side or both sides are tempted to strike first and the situation is unstable.

Antiballistic Missile Defenses

Since very little is known about the qualities of future antiballistic missile defenses, a simple expected-value representation of their effectiveness is used in this chapter. This expected-value model of ABM effectiveness is called "random subtractive defense." When the number of reentry vehicles (and decoys) is less than the number of available defensive interceptors, then all of the interceptors are aimed at all of the incoming objects. When the number of reentry vehicles (and decoys) is greater than the number of available defensive interceptors, then one interceptor is assigned to each incoming object and the objects in excess of the number of interceptors penetrate unopposed by the defenses.

The random subtractive defense approach for analyzing ballistic missile defenses can be extended to include the effect of decoys. When it is assumed that the decoys are perfect, or are perfect in misleading the defense, then the number of incoming objects is simply the number of reentry vehicles plus the number of decoys sent. A further refinement to this approach is to extend a previous analysis to examine decoy credibility.[11]

Bayesian Methods

Later in this chapter Bayesian methods will be employed to consider whether a commander would recommend launch-on-warning responses to an attack.[12] The recommendation is based on the commander improving his initial estimate of the likelihood of an attack (prior estimate) by observing arriving warning messages and upgrading or downgrading the confidence as to whether an attack is truly under way (posterior estimates). These estimates are a function of the probability that a warning message is generated indicating that there is an attack, the probability that a warning message is issued when there is no attack, the probability that no warning message is issued when there is an attack, and the probability that no warning message is generated when there is no attack. The a priori opinion of the commander that an attack is likely is expressed as a probability. Each time there is a warning or a no-warning message, a posterior probability is produced. This posterior probability becomes the input for the next cycle, which starts with the arrival of the next message. Thus, as messages are produced when an attack is detected, the opinion of the commander is modified by the receipt of information from the warning system. As more and more messages are received, the commander may gain more and more confidence that an attack is or is not under way. The equations in this model are used by some operations analysts and political scientists in their studies of how opinion or decision making is swayed by introducing data related to the decision to be made.[13]

FUTURE DETERRENCE AND ARMS REDUCTIONS

The purpose of this section is to examine potential effects on deterrence if further reductions in strategic nuclear weapons are a part of the future relationship between the United States and Russia. First-strike stability, a demanding measure of deterrence, is relevant to minimizing the likelihood of strategic nuclear war, and goes beyond the more traditional concept of central deterrence in that it is a two-sided measure. First-strike stability arises from the strategic force structures and force postures of the two sides, taking into account the vulnerability of each sides' forces as well as the number of weapons involved. First-strike stability relates to concepts enunciated almost four decades ago.[14] There is a concern on both sides about the vulnerability of nuclear forces and its effect on temptations to strike first. First, we treat first-strike stability under the two warhead limits of 2,500 and 800, and then turn to two effects that could lead to its deterioraton. The first effect arises if both sides agree to deploy a national missile defense. The second effect could arise if one or both sides were to arbitrarily decrease their alert rate or lessen their force postures.

An analysis of forces and postures outlined in the assumptions section of this chapter leads to the observation that first-strike stability is within reasonable limits:

Warhead Limit	First-Strike Stability Index
2,500	0.565
800	0.584

These values are somewhat lower than those that were the result of analyses of forces and postures that existed during the Cold War. These values are lower because it is assumed that the bomber forces on both sides are not on strip alert, as agreed to by Presidents Bush and Yeltsin. In spite of this effect, these values may be viewed as tolerable. Higher values could be the result of placing more weapon systems on each side on higher states of alert, or providing basing modes for future systems that featured lower vulnerabilities to rapid attacks.

Effect of Antiballistic Missile Defenses

First-strike stability is degraded by the deployment of ABM defenses. The rationale for this effect is that one side may be more likely to strike first if he believes that his ballistic missile defense can severely degrade the effectiveness of the retaliatory strike. The damage suffered by the first striker may be considered "tolerable" compared to what might happen without a ballistic missile defense. The first strike stability measure captures this effect. Figure 4.2 shows the results of the analyses when it is assumed that an ABM system is deployed by both sides. The figure indicates the first-strike stability as a function of the number of ABM interceptors deployed. At either warhead limit, it is clear that increasing the deployment of ABM interceptors results in increasing degradation of first-strike stability. Proponents of a limited national missile defense probably would argue that the degradation in first-strike stability is bearable if the ABM system is limited to 100 interceptors or so. This argument does indeed hold true if all the assumptions behind these analyses are met, but this may not be the case if assumptions are varied.

What would happen if both the United States and Russia were to devise countermeasures that would spoil the effectiveness of ABM systems? To examine this question, it has been assumed that Russia and the United States could deploy perfect decoys to lessen the effectiveness of either sides' ABM systems. In addition, it is assumed that there are twice as many decoys as reentry vehicles. The random subtractive defense model used in this analysis captures the essence of decoy effectiveness. First, the effect on first-strike stability will be analyzed. Subsequently, the credibility of the decoys may result in changing the ratio of decoys to reentry vehicles.

Figure 4.2
Effects of ABM Deployment

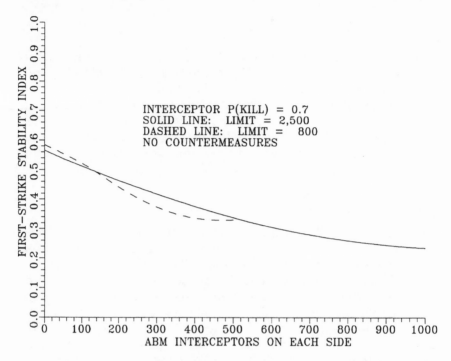

The results of both sides employing decoys to decrease the effectiveness of ABM defenses are shown in Figures 4.3 and 4.4. First-strike stability is shown as a function of the number of ABM interceptors deployed by each side with and without decoys. Figure 4.3 shows the results when the warhead limit is 2,500, and Figure 4.4 applies when the warhead limit is 800. The employment of perfect decoys degrades defense effectiveness and causes a much lower decrease in first-strike stability as the defenses are increased, compared to cases where decoys are not employed by either side. Under these circumstances, degradations in first-strike stability might be tolerable even if both sides were to deploy very large ABM systems. However, one could argue that if large ABM systems are so easily countered it would seem foolish to deploy them in the first place. Such an argument has great merit when confrontations between superpowers and large nuclear exchanges are involved. For lesser confrontations with rogue nations, each of the superpowers may decide that they need limited ABM defenses to counter limited attacks or accidental launches of ballistic missiles. Again, this observation is based on the validity of "nominal" assumptions, and these could change.

Figure 4.3
Effect of ABM (START III)

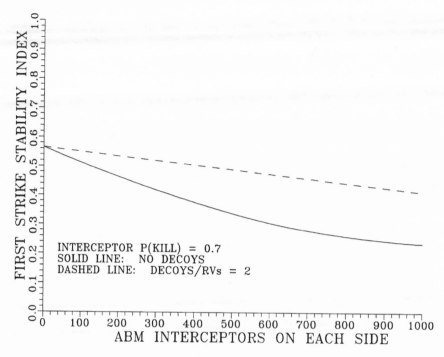

INTERCEPTOR P(KILL) = 0.7
SOLID LINE: NO DECOYS
DASHED LINE: DECOYS/RVs = 2

ABM INTERCEPTORS ON EACH SIDE

One critical issue related to ABM defenses is the capability to discriminate between reentry vehicles and decoys. In this analysis the discrimination issue is addressed by examining decoy credibility. If discrimination is perfect, the the decoy credibility is zero. If the defense cannot discriminate between reentry vehicles and decoys, then the decoy credibility is 1.0. In the design of ABM systems, every effort is made to minimize the probability that a decoy is perceived as a reentry vehicle, and the probability that a reentry vehicle is perceived as a decoy. This discrimination capability is often performed by examining the characteristics of all reentering objects in various spectra, such as visible light, infrared, radar, and so forth. The proof of any such capability rests finally on test results. Testing results may vary considerably depending on how well the objects used replicate the decoys and reentry vehicles of the expected attacker. The defender employs the expected perceptions in the allocation of interceptors to objects he believes are reentry vehicles. If the stockpile of interceptors is large compared to the number of perceived reentry vehicles, the defender may hedge his bets by aiming interceptors at perceived de-

Figure 4.4
Effect of ABM (Limit = 800 Warheads)

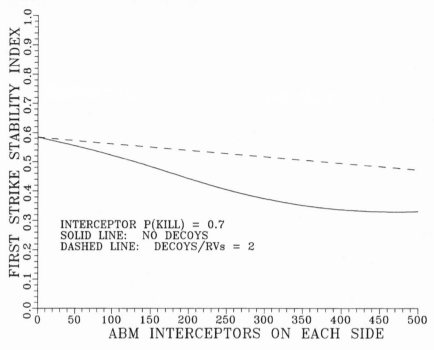

coys on the chance that they are really reentry vehicles. The ingredients of a previous analysis take all of these possibilities into account.[15]

Since decoys may not be perfect, how many decoys should be sent to maintain the same probability of penetrating the ABM defenses? Figure 4.5 shows the ratio of decoys needed to meet this goal as a function of decoy credibility. The curve is based on the assumption that there are twice as many perfect decoys as reentry vehicles. As the decoy credibility decreases, then the attacker should send more decoys. The trick for the attacker is to properly assess the discrimination capabilities of the opposing ABM defense, an uncertain estimate at best.

There are large uncertainties for both the attacker and defender. The attacker must somehow make a reasonable estimate of the defender's discrimination capability to decide on the number of decoys he may need. The defender may have no preconceived notion as to what characteristics of the attacker's decoys should be examined to decide on a reasonable design for the ABM system. Most enthusiasts for a national missile defense agree that discrimination would not be perfect. Some analysts maintain that discrimination would be far from perfect and

Figure 4.5
Ratio of Decoys to RVs Needed to Offset ABM Discrimination

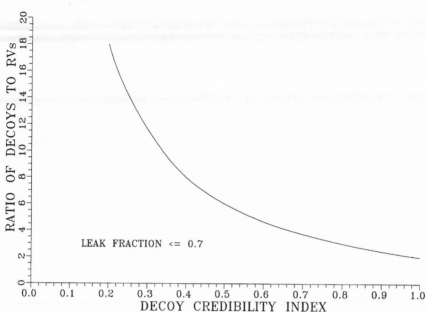

decoys might be mistaken for reentry vehicles in most engagements. The author tends to side with the latter group of observers. The exact nature of decoys used by either the United States or Russia, or even a rogue nation, may be difficult to determine ahead of any crisis or potential nuclear confrontation. The role of technical-intelligence capabilities would be crucial in even partially resolving such uncertainties.

Effect of Lower Alert Rates

Lower alert rates or degraded postures of strategic nuclear forces can lead to lower values of first-strike stability and a potential diminution of deterrence. The first striker could be tempted to attack, since he would be fairly confident of destroying a large fraction of the defender's nuclear warheads, which are not on alert and therefore much more vulnerable than if they were on alert and better protected from attack.

The reason for future concern over this issue rests on an important economic factor: the expense of maintaining nuclear forces on alert, particularly for the Russians. Recent revelations by the U.S. Navy and intelligence agencies indicate that at times the Russians may have none of their strategic missile-carrying submarines at sea.[16] Sometimes, two submarines are kept on pier-side alert. In addition, many of the Russian military have not received their pay. Thus, Russian economic problems may force their military establishment to lower the alert rates for nuclear forces far below the "nominal" values assumed earlier in Table 4.1.

What is the effect of lowering alert rates for Russian nuclear forces? To examine this question, we vary the number of Russian strategic submarines (SSBN) at sea under each limit on strategic nuclear warheads—START III (2,500 warheads) and a limit of 800 warheads. The bombers are assumed not to be on strip alert in accordance with earlier agreements, and we assume that silo-based ICBMs would always be on alert but would not be launched on warning. Figure 4.6 shows the results of the analyses where the number of submarines at sea is varied. For a limit of 2,500 warheads, there would be 692 warheads on alert under nominal assumptions. If no Typhoons were at sea, then there would be 372 warheads on alert, and where no Typhoon or Delfin SSBNs were at sea, then there would be 244 ICBM warheads on alert. Under these variations, the first-strike stability would decrease from 0.56 to 0.12 as indicated on the right-hand side of Figure 4.6.

First-strike stability would decrease in a similar manner under a warhead limit of 800. For the lower warhead limit it was assumed that there would be three Delfin SSBNs at sea under nominal assumptions. The effect of decreasing this number to one SSBN and then to none is shown in Figure 4.6. In addition, the effect of taking the mobile ICBMs (RS-12M) off alert (i.e., returning them to their garrisons), is also indicated.

The overall impact of such decreases in alert or at-sea rates is dramatic, and such low values of first-strike stability could be a cause for concern about the relationship between the United States and Russia. However, some might view even the indicated decreases in first-strike stability with equanimity, since the analysis indicates that it is the United States that would be tempted to strike first under the assumptions of decreased at-sea rates. Many political observers might be convinced that the United States would never strike first under present post–Cold War political conditions. Such a conviction may not be shared by the present or future Russian leadership.

Geopolitical Stability and Alert Rates

To many analysts, geopolitical stability seems to be a nonquantifiable measure of the political relations between two nations; in this case, between the United States and Russia. While we do not propose a definition of geopolitical stability, we suggest that there are some indicators of geopolitical stability. At the very least, the indicators of geopolitical stability would seem to include the following:

Figure 4.6
Effects of Lowering Russian Alert Rates

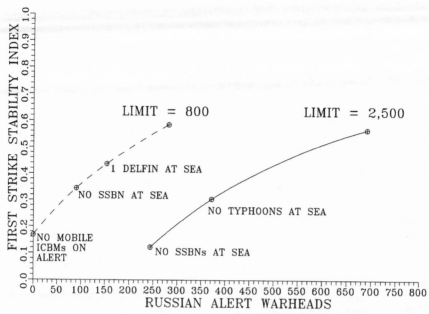

1. The state of relations and understandings on central issues of the two countries.
2. The degree of amicability concerning commerce and trade.
3. The extent of diplomatic differences concerning noncentral issues.
4. The perception or extent of threatening intentions or capabilities.

Examples of these indicators might include support of the ABM Treaty, expansion of NATO, START I, and START II (central issues), the extent to which American and Russian companies are forming industrial partnerships (commerce and trade), and potential agreement or contention about Third World activities such as nuclear activities in North Korea, or the state of affairs in the Middle East (noncentral issues). With regard to the extent of threatening intentions or capabilities, one indicator selected for this analysis is the degree of relaxation of military tensions; namely, the nonalert status of strategic nuclear forces on each side.

How far are the United States and Russia willing to go in placing their strategic forces on nonalert status? The approach to examining reductions in alert rates for strategic forces is continuous in nature. In this approach the alert rate of each element of the strategic forces on both sides is reduced gradually so as to preserve the role of each element of the two triads of forces. As the nonalert rate increases for each of the suggested warhead limits, each element of the strategic forces is reduced in proportion to the total warhead limit. With this approach, portions of the submarine fleet and bomber force are removed from at-sea or strip-alert postures as the overall fraction on alert is decreased. For the Russian side, the same proportional reductions apply, but are appropriate for their mobile ICBMs.

The results of this approach to increasing the nonalert rate of strategic forces are shown in Figure 4.7. In this figure, first-strike stability is shown as a function of the fraction of forces with a variable alert rate on a nonalert status. When this measure is high, nearly 1.0, then geopolitical stability is indicated as being high, assuming that all of the other indicators have been assessed as being within acceptable bounds. Since it could be difficult for an outside observer to discriminate between silo-based ICBMs that are on alert and those that are not, these results include the assumption that all ICBMs in silos are always on alert. These results also include an assumption that the alert or at-sea rates for bombers, mobile ICBMs, and submarines are set initially at 100 percent and then decreased proportionally as the nonalert rate is increased. At the end point, a nonalert rate of 1.0, only the silo-based ICBMs are assumed to be on alert.

Figure 4.7 shows that when the nonalert rate is low, the first-strike stability is extremely high, but does degrade as the nonalert rate is increased for all of the warhead limits considered here. At lowered warhead limits the first-strike stability is lower at nonalert rates in excess of 0.4 than would be estimated to prevail under START II. The main point to be drawn from this figure is to show how far political amity may be pushed in terms of forcewide nonalert rates without upsetting first-strike stability. Increases in nonalert rates for strategic forces may be a method of assuring geopolitical stability, but does provide some drawbacks in terms of first-strike stability, and this trade-off is illustrated. Lower nonalert rates may be needed at lower warhead limits to preserve an acceptable level of first-strike stability.

Figure 4.7 does not illustrate the effects of a reversal of alert rates should geopolitical stability be perceived as decreasing because of other nonquantitative trends, such as deteriorating diplomatic or economic relations or growing disagreements between Russia and the United States. In the face of such deteriorations, either the United States or Russia may decide to lower nonalert rates (increase alert) of their strategic forces. Intelligence organizations may detect the increases in strategic alert rates. Their projections could be in error or misinterpreted. In an extreme case, detected increases in alert rates could be interpreted as one side or the other preparing for a first strike. While plac-

Figure 4.7
First-Strike Stability with Two-Sided Nonalert Rates

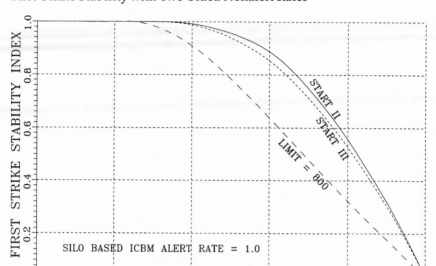

ing more forces on higher states of alert would improve first-strike stability, such steps could serve to lessen geopolitical stability and could raise false alarms for either side. Diplomatic consultation between the two sides might aid in calming such situations, but such exchanges may not resolve uncertainties in perceptions and interpretations to the satisfaction of the participants. While placing more and more strategic nuclear forces on nonalert status may reflect geopolitical stability, withdrawing them from nonalert status may set off alarms among the leadership of either or both sides.

From this analysis it appears likely that first-strike and geopolitical stability can be preserved at tolerable levels at reduced warhead levels beyond the terms of START II, even though the objectives of promoting political stability and preserving first-strike stability are not usually in accord. However, this analysis does not account for the arsenals or the political goals of other nations. At very low levels of nuclear forces, any confrontational situation may become multipolar in nature. If all nations eventually come to the view that nuclear weapons are unusable, then deep reductions in the nuclear arsenals of the United States and Russia may be possible.

CONSIDERATIONS OF LAUNCH ON WARNING

When the strategic nuclear weapons of the United States and Russia are reduced, a potential risk that could be encountered would be the dangers inherent in a "launch-on-warning" or "launch-under-attack" tactic. Such tactics have been considered by many analysts and decision makers since the dawn of the nuclear age. The emphasis of this discussion will be placed on the tactic of launch on warning. Until recently, U.S. public policy on launch on warning has always been vague, indicating to a potential attacker that he might face such a response or he might not. Motivation for considering such a doctrine, its feasibility, and commentary are offered here.

Motivation for Launch on Warning

The basic motivation on the part of some military and political strategists has been the possibility of using nuclear warheads before they are destroyed by an enemy attack, implementing the familiar adage, "Use it or lose it." The use of this tactic is a step to increase strategic survivability. Such a tactic has been employed for the bomber force. Some bombers are placed on strip alert so they might escape before nuclear warheads impact on the United States. Unlike ballistic missiles, bombers can be recalled if the warning signals and messages are later deemed to be in error.

With regard to U.S. ICBMs, there has always been some concern over their potential vulnerability, particularly those housed in underground silos. During the 1980s these concerns grew dramatically and were often expressed with the term, "window of vulnerability." At that time, the former Soviet Union possessed over 300 SS-18 ICBMs, each armed with ten reentry vehicles. Intelligence estimates of the accuracy of Soviet ICBMs combined with the range of uncertainties in the hardness of U.S. silos resulted in a genuine concern about the survival of the United States ICBM force based in Minuteman silos. Both Minuteman and the Peace Keeper ICBMs could be considered high-value targets to an attacker because they carry multiple warheads, three for Minuteman and ten for the Peace Keeper.

The bounds of the window of vulnerability are functions of attacking warheads and silo vulnerability. The hardness of the silos is one factor, and the delivery accuracy (circular probable error [CEP]) is another. Minuteman silos are believed to be designed to withstand overpressures of 2,000 psi, but might withstand as much as 4,000 psi under an optimistic view.[17] The probable errors of the Soviet delivery systems are assumed to be between 300 and 600 ft. Under these assumptions, the window of vulnerability is bounded between single-shot kill probabilities of 0.99 in the worst case and 0.68 for the optimistic view. If the Soviets were to target two warheads on these silos, then the probability of silo survival would range between 0.000049 and 0.103. Neither of these values were considered reassuring to most analysts. Under the tactic of launch on warning, the survivability of an ICBM is equal to its availability rate for launching, or about 0.9 (maybe higher) instead of 0.1 or less if it were not launched before the arrival of attacking reentry vehicles. Overall, the number of ICBMs launched out of a force of 1,000 missiles after an attack would be on the order of zero to 100, but would be 900 or more if the launch-on-warning tactic were to be employed. These estimates overlook some important operational matters, such as the implications of false warning signals, and, secondarily, the timing of the arrival of U.S. warheads and other constraints that normally would be in effect in an operational war plan.

Feasibility of Launch on Warning

Regarding the feasibility of implementing a launch-on-warning tactic, two important questions must be addressed. How confident can we be that the attack is under way? Is there enough time available to implement launch on warning? The first question will be addressed by examining the effectiveness of warning systems and commanders in assessing the probability that an attack is under way, using extensions to Bayesian statistics. The second question will be addressed by bounding the time available to make decisions and send out launch orders.

Warning-System Messages and Confidence Levels

In this analysis our assumptions are made to address situations that are less than ideal. Under ideal conditions it is assumed that every message indicates that an attack is under way. In an attempt to capture more realism, it will be assumed that some messages will be generated indicating that no attack is under way even when the converse is true. Since warning-system performance may be less than ideal, the probabilities of warning and no warning given an attack will be varied. This analysis includes the effect of erroneous messages (no attack is under way even when it is) by employing Monte Carlo techniques. Using this approach, a message indicating that no attack is under way (even when it is) is generated when a random draw is less than some expected error rate. In this instance, it is assumed that the threshhold is the nondetection of an attack. The nondetection threshhold is set at 0.05 to show the effects on the number of messages needed to assure high confidence that an attack is under way. Under the random draw of a fraction, if the fraction is 0.05 or less a message indicating that no attack is under way will be generated. If the random fraction is greater than 0.05 a message will be generated indicating that an attack is under way. These assumptions seem to describe a fairly efficient warning system. The results of the analysis will be based on 100 Monte Carlo runs.

The first example is based on the assumption that a commander is predisposed to the probability of an attack of 0.05, a small but finite value. On the average, it would take about six messages to assure high confidence (0.99 or more) that an attack really is imminent. In simulations such as this one, there may be streaks of good or bad luck. The generation of warning that an attack involving nuclear weapons is under way may be a very uncommon occurrence. Thus, 100 trials may not be an appropriate value to assure decision makers of what might happen at sporadic times when an attack is suspected. Streaks of good and bad luck may seem extreme, but they are possible within the statisical bounds of this analysis. Figure 4.8 indicates both extremes for this particular example. The best case of 100 runs results when every message generated indicates that an attack is under way, and is what one might expect under ideal conditions. On the other hand, the dashed line shows an extreme result in the other direction. The first message causes the commander to increase his expectation of an attack, but the mixture of attack and no-attack messages that follow illustrate the effect of a streak of bad luck. In the bad-luck case, about eight messages are needed to achieve high confidence that an attack is under way.

What would be the effect if warning-system performance were less than the efficiency just assumed? The next examples of the Monte Carlo simulations are based on the assumptions that the probability of warning given an attack is now 0.7 (not 0.95) and the probability of no warning given an attack is 0.3 (not 0.05). These assumptions are used to illustrate the effects of a potential deterioration in the performance of warning systems.

First, we assume that a commander is predisposed to believe that the probability of an attack is low, 0.05. Under this assumed predisposition, the average of 100 runs indicates that receipt of forty messages will not result in an attack expectation of 0.99 or greater. Figure 4.9 indicates this average along with streaks of good and bad luck. The streak of good luck is based on one run where success messages were error free at first, but followed by a few messages indicating that no attack was under way. There is a slight wavering of confidence when ten messages are received. The curve corresponding to the streak of bad luck indicates what the author believes to be the worst case of the 100 runs. Even after the receipt of forty messages, the expectation of attack never ex-

Figure 4.8
Attack Warning Results (Simulation)

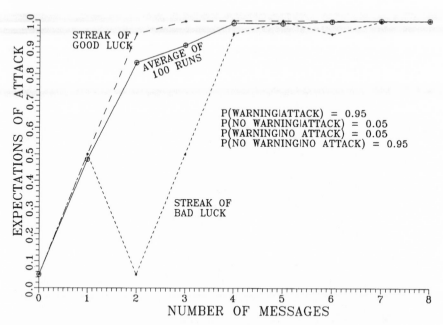

ceeds 0.8. The risk that such a string of messages could occur may tend to discourage high-level decision makers, whether they are considering the implementation of a launch-on-warning tactic.

One could argue that raising the commander's predisposition as to the likelihood of an attack might improve or compensate for low reliabilities in a warning system. To illustrate this possiblity, it is assumed that the commander's opinion concerning the likelihood of an attack is increased from 0.05 to 0.5. Figure 4.10 indicates the results. On average, about thirty-five to forty messages are needed to achieve some high degree of confidence, but somewhat less than 0.99 in this particular simulation. With a streak of good luck, about eight messages would result in a high confidence that an attack was under way. Under a run of bad luck, a high confidence that an attack is under way is never achieved, and it is more likely that a launch on warning would not be ordered even though some might believe it to be a mandatory response. Thus, the results of these simulations indicate that even a heightened state of alert on the part of the commander will not ameliorate problems that lie in the performance of a warning system.

Several important parameters are not considered in analyses of this type. No consideration is given to the effect of reports based on mul-

Figure 4.9
Examples of Attack Warning Simulation

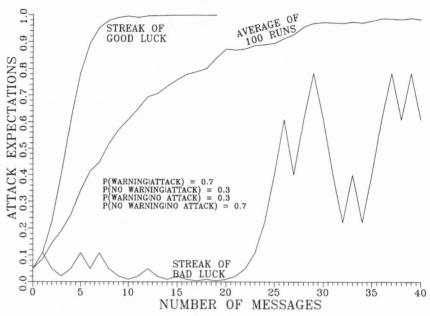

tiple phenomenologies (radar, infrared, visible light, seismic, or other sensors). No consideration is given to the number of warheads in the assumed attack. These parameters contribute to the validity and reliability of the outputs of any warning system. Unreliability in sensors may have an effect on the efficiency of the warning system. The size of a supposed attack could have an enormous impact on the reaction of a commander. Is only one missile involved, or are there 100 MIRVed missiles approaching? Thus, this analysis should be considered as scratching the surface of the problem. On the other hand, no matter how many tests are conducted and how much confidence is placed on the design of a warning system, we may never really know or appreciate how good or bad its performance in a single trial may be. Command exercises, no matter how carefully designed, may not uncover flaws in the total warning system.

Determining the time available to implement the launch-on-warning tactic is needed to assess it feasibility. In performing this assessment, the analysis will focus on Russian warning devices. If the Russians were to worry about U.S. ICBM attacks, they would need to rely on their space-based launch-detection system. The time available for a launch-on-warning decision would be the flight time of an ICBM, about

Figure 4.10
Examples of Attack Warning Simulation

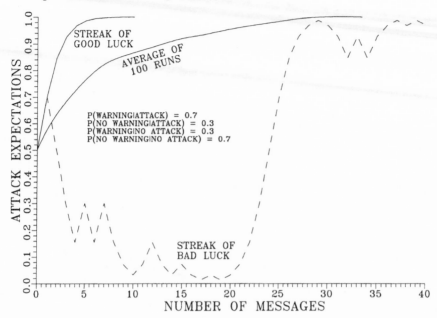

twenty-five to thirty-five minutes. Shorter times would be involved if the first round of an attack were initiated by sea-launched ballistic missiles. Some have suggested that the Russians might have a space-based system that would observe the launch of these missiles.[18] If so, the time available would be on the order of the SLBM flight time. Recent reports indicate that Russian space-based launch-detection systems may not be available or that their effectiveness is diminishing because replacement satellites are not being launched to fill in for satellites that have failed.[19] In the worst case, SLBMs could be observed only by the Russian early warning radar systems.

Severe timing constraints would prevail if the Russians were expecting an attack employing SLBMs launched off the coast of Newfoundland and aimed at Moscow. The Russians might have only their radar to detect such an attack. Figure 4.11 indicates the radar parameters, range, elevation angle, and azimuth angle of the flight path of the warheads involved. From this figure, approximately nine minutes would be available (at most) for a decision to launch on warning, if all of the Russian ICBMs and in-port SLBMs were at their highest readiness condition and local commanders were assumed to be able to execute a launch order instantaneously. Such assumptions may not be

Figure 4.11
Example of Radar Tracking Data

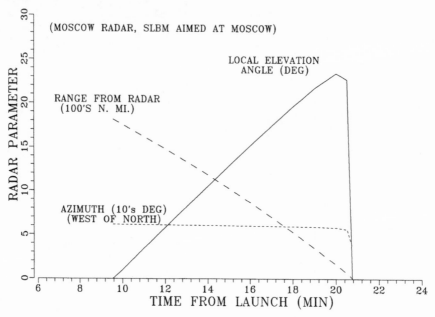

realistic. A warning report might not be generated at the first detection of the warheads. Time would be needed to assemble the requisite data. ICBMs ordered to launch in a prompt manner may not be ready to do so. The time taken to reach a high confidence level that an attack is under way may be longer than expected. Other factors not considered here may also interfere with implementation of launch on warning, such as weapon-arrival timing, avoidance of fratricide between reentry vehicles near impact, and limiting the number of silo doors that are open at any given moment.

One incident directly involving Russian reaction to the detection of a potential attack has been described.[20] The incident involved the launch of a sounding rocket from Andoya, an island just off the northern Norwegian coastline. Russian sensors did detect the event. High-level decision makers were assembled and discussed the consequences of reacting to a supposed attack or not reacting. In the end, no Russian missiles were launched on warning. The overall warning system appeared to have worked, since the launch was detected by radars, and the procedures involving high-level decision makers did work successfully. One Russian problem appeared to be that they were not aware of an advisory message to the effect that such a launch operation was to take place. The message apparently did not reach the higher levels of command. Thus, we conclude that the Russian system probably was tested under realistic conditions, and portions of the overall system may have been found wanting. Luckily, or because hasty decisions were avoided, or because Russian leaders were predisposed to believe that the United States would not attack, the outcome of the affair ended without involvement in nuclear combat. The discrepancies that appeared during the sounding-rocket incident appear to have been deficiencies in command and communication procedures rather than failures of sensors to detect the launch and relay the data to appropriate headquarters. Russian radar detected the launch, but higher levels of the Russian government failed to receive or pay attention to diplomatic notifications prior to the event.

With regard to feasibility, it may not be possible to confidently rely on a launch-on-warning tactic. Under the worst case, an attack by a sea-launched ballistic missile, the time of flight of such a missile is short. In the calculations presented here, about eight to ten minutes might form the time frame for a launch on warning to be implemented. As was shown, anywhere from about six to forty or so messages warning of an attack might be needed to assure high confidence that an attack was under way under the assumption of a degraded warning system and a commander's low disposition to assume that an attack was probable. If the frequency of warning messages were high, about one every thirty seconds, then launch on warning might be feasible if six to ten messages were involved under "ideal" conditions. Under more realistic conditions, thirty or so messages might be needed to assure high confidence that an attack was under way. Under these assumptions, implementation of launch on warning would not seem feasible. If the interval between warning messages generated on the basis of various sensors were longer, then the feasibility of launch on warning would be tenuous at best. Other factors also must be considered. These would include the timing of the launch response (the length of time needed to launch an appreciable fraction of the ballistic missile force, ICBMs and SLBMs), and the state of alert of the missiles involved in such a launch. All these factors are uncertain, particularly in the case of a Russian response. One other factor not considered here is the reaction of the head of state, either in the United States or Russia, and the timing of his or her decision. Overall, our assessment is that launch on warning seems easy, cheap, and neat, but extremely dangerous on all of the counts just mentioned, including the accidental destruction of a substantial portion of modern civilization.

Finally, the current policy of the United States appears to be to not launch on warning. In the past the launch-on-warning policy has purposely been left somewhat vague, thus indicating to the former Soviet Union that it might or might not face a launch-on-warning response if it chose to strike first. More recently, however, Robert Bell made the following statement in discussing a Presidential Decision Directive (PDD-60, November 1997).[21]

With respect to strategic nuclear deterrence, the PDD reaffirms our fundamental committment to maintain a strategic nuclear posture across a triad of strategic forces, a robust posture that is not dependent on a launch-on-warning planning assumption, and that includes secure reserve forces and survivability sufficient to allow you to confirm that a nuclear weapon has actually detonated on American soil before you would have to face the retaliatory decision.

With regard to the Russians, the only available experience concerning launch on warning has been positive. When an unexpected launch occurred near the Norwegian coast, high-level decision makers did not order their forces to launch on warning in retaliation. Whether or not such a positive action on their part would be taken in the future remains quite uncertain. Steps are being taken to share U.S. warning information with the Russians to avoid such situations, but the outcome and implementation of such steps is not a certainty.[22]

BREAKING OUT OF TREATY AGREEMENTS

In the defense and arms control community there is often a worry about the consequences of a sudden abrogation of an arms control agreement. Several possibilities of such events are considered in this discussion. If there is a breakout, the concern is that the number of warheads can be increased dramatically. Some fear that such increases in armament will result in one side suddenly becoming dominant, and that any form of stability would be upset. In this chapter it will be assumed that the number of weapon delivery systems remains constant when one or both sides break out of an agreement. It is assumed that the number of warheads carried by ICBMs or SLBMs will be increased surreptitiously. This assumption seems consistent with the possibility of cheating if an overall accord on inspection and verification were less than complete and thorough. In this examination, the two levels of nuclear-weapon arsenals used earlier will be addressed: 2,500 and 800 warheads possessed by each side.

Assumptions Concerning Forces

For the purposes of this analysis it is assumed that the number of warheads carried by ICBMs and SLBMs could be increased. The number of warheads carried by bombers is assumed not to change if one side or both were to break out from an agreement.

Under the assumptions made earlier in this chapter, land-based ICBMs are limited to one warhead apiece. SLBMs carry an agreed number of reentry vehicles. The incremental changes assumed for the analysis of a breakout are displayed in Table 4.3. In this table the increased payloads of ballistic missiles are shown under the START III accords and for a lower limit of 800 warheads. The assumptions behind each of the increases in the number of reentry vehicles is based on reports or initial design objectives of the original ballistic missiles assumed in this chapter.

If such changes were to occur, the number of nuclear warheads on either side would more than double. Such a suddenly emerging threat could be of great concern to both political decision makers and military strategists, if they were aware of such changes.

Table 4.2
Incremental Warhead Increases for a Breakout

System	Warheads per Ballistic Missile	
	No Breakout	Breakout
United States, START III		
Minuteman	1 RV per ICBM	3 RV per ICBM
Trident	4 RV per SLBM	12 RV per SLBM
Total Warheads	2500	5780
Russia, START III		
RS-18	1 RV per ICBM	6 RV per ICBM
RS-12	1 RV per ICBM	4 RV per ICBM
Typhoon	8 RV per SLBM	10 RV per SLBM
Delfin	4 RV per SLBM	10 RV per SLBM
Total Warheads	2500	5434
United States, Limit = 800		
Minuteman	1 RV per ICBM	3 RV per ICBM
Trident	2 RV per SLBM	8 RV per SLBM
Total Warheads	800	2192
Russia, Limit = 800		
RS-12	1 RV per ICBM	4 RV per ICBM
Delfin	4 RV per SLBM	10 RV per SLBM
Total Warheads	800	2360

Damage Levels When Either Side Strikes First

Damage to the attacker and defender are employed as a measures to examine cases where Russia might break out of an arms control accord. This measure is the fraction of valued assets damaged should either Russia or the United States break out. These measures are purely one sided, but show the implications of a breakout in stark terms. Again, limits of 2,500 and 800 warheads are the subjects of the analyses. Table 4.3 shows the damage inflicted on U.S. valued assets when Russia strikes first and the damage to Russian valued assets when the United States strikes first. The second half of the table shows the damage to the first striker, either Russia or the United States.

If Russia were to break out of the limits of 2,500 or 800 warheads and strike first, then the damage to the United States would increase substantially compared to the no-breakout case. This effect would be the benefit to Russia of breaking out. If the United States should detect the Russian breakout and increase their warheads as indicated in Table 4.3, then the damage to the United States would increase by a small amount.

Russia would also have to consider the damage inflicted by a U.S. retaliatory strike. When Russia breaks out, the damage to Russia because of a return strike by the United States decreases by a small amount for either warhead limit, another benefit to Russia. However, if the United States also breaks out from the agreements, then there would be a substantial increase in the damage to Russia. This increase would be a penalty to Russia if it believed that the United States could detect a breakout and follow suit.

If Russia were to break out, and Russia were to strike first, then the damage to the United States would increase by at least one-third to more than double the amount that would be experienced without any breakout. This increase would be a benefit for Russia and a penalty to the United States. Should the United States and Russia both break out, then the damage levels to the United States, if it were struck first, would be about the same as if only Russia were to break out of their agreements.

Overall, there would be benefits to Russia if it were to break out, but only if the United States failed to detect the cheating and did not increase its warhead count in a similar manner. Should the United States detect the cheating and increase its warhead count, then both Russia and the United States would face very high damage levels no matter who struck first. Neither side might wish to face such consequences of a breakout, and both nations might be deterred from striking first, or even from breaking out of arms-reduction agreements.

In the final analysis, a Russian breakout from warhead limits of 2,500

Table 4.3
Damage Levels Under Breakout

Limit	No Breakout	Russia Breaks Out	Both Break Out
	Russia Strikes First, Damage to the United States		
2500	0.687	0.928	0.946
800	0.356	0.799	0.863
	United States Strikes First, Damage to Russia		
2500	0.777	0.703	0.948
800	0.469	0.449	0.750
	Russia Strikes First, Damage to Russia		
2500	0.702	0.632	0.955
800	0.312	0.305	0.687
	United States Strikes First, Damage to United States		
2500	0.388	0.556	0.518
800	0.253	0.573	0.572

or 800 may depend not so much on the increases (or minor decreases) in damage as on the absolute number of warheads that would be available for a Russian first strike against the United States, particularly if such a breakout went undetected and the United States did not respond in some manner. The U.S. response need not be an increase in their number of warheads, but might consist of preventive measures to assure that a Russian breakout could not occur. Such measures could include putting more warheads on alert, or demanding very strict terms of an arms control agreement (i.e., very intrusive inspections of ballistic missile payloads). Similar inspection regimes would also apply to the bomber forces, but those regimes were assumed before initiating this analysis.

SUMMARY AND OBSERVATIONS

The purpose of this chapter has been to provide insights into opportunities and some of the risks involving future reductions in the strategic nuclear arsenals of Russia and the United States. Whether or not such reductions are achieved will be dependent on the future leadership of the two countries. Their perspectives and policies toward nuclear arms will be determining factors. Reductions such as those examined here could entail risk, and some of these risks were briefly examined. On the whole, this author believes that substantial reductions in strategic nuclear warheads in both the United States and Russia could be accomplished without reducing the degree of deterrence provided by the large stockpiles of weapons that currently exist. Risks can be minimized or controlled by implementing arms-reduction accords that include measures to assure transparency, accountability, and adherence to agreements for both sides.

The reductions considered in this chapter were indicative of a near-term opportunity, START III, and a future opportunity, a limit of 800 warheads on both sides. Between these two exemplary bounds there may be intermediate steps on the way to substantial reductions, which were not considered in this discussion. The intent of the present analyses was to examine an example of a warhead limit somewhat less than 1,000 warheads in an attempt to illuminate some future prospects and potential problems that might arise or that must be accomodated. The author believes that if the future were to involve reductions below 800 warheads each for the United States and Russia, then present methods of examining deterrence and first-strike stability will need to be expanded to include the effects of other national policies and stockpiles of nuclear weapons. The analyses presented in this chapter have been limited strictly to two-sided reductions of nuclear weapons between the United States and Russia.

First-Strike Stability and Arms Reductions

One purpose of this chapter has been to provide perspective on deep reductions in the number of strategic nuclear warheads possessed by the United States and Russia. This perspective has been based on two distinct quantitative measures. The first is a crucial aspect of deterrence, particularly in a crisis: first-strike stability. The second is one indicator of peacetime geopolitical stability, the fraction of strategic nuclear weapons not on alert status.

First-strike stability is a measure of the lack of incentive for either side to strike first. First-strike stability will decrease, or incentives to strike first will rise, under the influence of two major parameter variations: the posture of forces and the deployment of antiballistic missile defenses on both sides. As the force posture or alert status of forces is decreased, then first-strike stability decreases. In this chapter, reductions in force posture were examined by assuming a "nominal" alert rate for both sides, and then varied by reducing the number of Russian missile-carrying submarines at sea. Such trends have been observed in Russian at-sea rates, and probably are the result of economic difficulties within Russia and their impact on military forces. Under significant reductions in Russian at-sea rates, first-strike stability was seriously degraded.

Another factor that could degrade first-strike stability is the deployment of antiballistic missile defenses by both the United States and Russia. The impact of such deployments was illustrated for both warhead reductions examined. In both cases, the deployment of more and more interceptors steadily decreased first-strike stability. At the extreme limits of interceptor deployment considered here, the first striker's ABM reduced the damage inflicted by a retaliatory strike, thus increasing incentives to strike first. A major shift in this trend was observed when perfect decoys were deployed by both sides on their ballistic missiles. The effect of decoys was to increase the effectiveness of retaliatory strikes by spoiling the effectiveness of ABM systems, thus reducing the degradations in first-strike stability caused by introducing strategic defenses. If decoys are not completely credible, as first assumed, then more decoys would need to be employed. Small deployments of ABM defense, 100 interceptors or less, would result in small decreases in first-strike stability, and permit some degree of protection from attacks by so-called rogue nations. Even though the ABM Treaty permits each side to deploy 100 interceptors, Article I bans the deployment of a national ballistic missile defense. Changes to the ABM Treaty would be needed to accomodate even limited deployments of national ballistic missile defenses. The two important parametric variations which would lead to degradation in first-strike stability were lowering of alert rates and deployment of strategic defenses.

Not all of the elements of geopolitical stability are quantifiable; some remain a matter of perception by leaders of the United States and Russia. At the least, the indicators of geopolitical stability would seem to include (1) the state of relations and understandings on central issues between the two countries, (2) the degree of amicability concerning commerce and trade, (3) the extent of diplomatic differences concerning noncentral issues, and (4) the perception or extent of threatening intentions or capabilities. The indicator of geopolitical stability selected in this analysis concerned perceptions related to threat, or the degree of relaxation of military tensions; namely, the nonalert status of strategic nuclear forces on each side.

In past years geopolitical stability has seemingly increased when both the United States and Russia agreed to remove strategic bombers from continuous strip alert. The agreement to do so was perceived as an act of goodwill and willingness to reduce military tension after the end of the Cold War. Such actions did decrease first-strike stability, but were deemed acceptable in favor of promoting geopolitical stability and the display of intentions toward establishing a more peaceful relationship. How far would both sides be willing to go in reducing alert rates? One result of the present analysis indicates the trade-off between first-strike stability and the fraction of forces on nonalert status. In general, substantial fractions of nuclear forces can be removed from alert status while preserving a high degree of first-strike stability. When all forces are placed on alert, first-strike stability is at its upper limit. Decreases in first-strike stability begin to occur when about half of the nuclear forces on both sides are placed on a nonalert status. At this point first-strike stability also begins to degrade as the limits on nuclear arsenals are decreased. For the condition where 80 percent of forces are on nonalert status, the assumed terms of a START III treaty may be considered acceptable, or at least marginally so. First-strike stability under an arsenal limit of 800 warheads could be judged as being too low for comfort.

Overall, higher fractions of nuclear forces can be placed on nonalert status when warhead limits are high than might be tolerated under conditions when the warhead limit is low, if the goal is to preserve some constant level of first-strike stability. The reader is cautioned that this indicator, the fraction of forces on nonalert status, is but one aspect of geopolitical stability, and that other elements must surely enter into considerations by political leaders on how far they might agree to procede in taking strategic nuclear forces off alert status, particularly when considering deep reductions in force size.

The objectives in promoting geopolitical stability and in preserving first-strike stability are not always in accord. From this limited analysis, political objectives in providing peaceful relations may call for tolerance in terms of reduced first-strike stability. On the other hand, efforts to restore first-strike stability after initially taking nuclear forces off alert status may be viewed as an alarming degradation of political factors if a crisis were to occur. A state of balance may not be enduring over time, and factors beyond the scope of this analysis may be more important.

From this analysis it appears very likely that first-strike stability and geopolitical stability can be preserved at tolerable levels even at reduced warhead levels beyond those in START II. However, this analysis does not account for the arsenals or political goals of other nations, such as China, North Korea, Britain, or France, to mention but a few other potential contenders. At very low levels of nuclear forces, any confrontational situation may become multipolar in nature.

Launch on Warning

The issue of whether nuclear-armed ballistic missiles should be launched on warning of an attack has been resurrected from time to time, usually as a result of advances in reducing weapon-system delivery errors. Subsequently, such a tactic has been perceived to be extremely dangerous and discarded. However, such dangers could become critical at lower levels of nuclear-weapon inventories.

Launch on warning is often perceived as an easy way of compensating for increased vulnerability of basing schemes for ballistic missiles. Perceived lower delivery errors have often led to perceived lowering of the survivability of silos or docked submarines. One "solution" suggested has been the implementation of a launch-on-warning tactic. Under this tactic, the survivability of a ballistic missile would be its availability rate (0.9 or so) rather than its probability of surviving the severe damage from an attacker's nuclear warhead, a reflection of the "use it or lose it" syndrome.

Whether ballistic missiles could be launched on warning is dependent on the solutions to the many problems involved. How sure can a commander be that a devastating attack is under way? Is there enough time available to make a profound and irreversible decision and transmit it to all ballistic missile bases? Could a large fraction of the ballistic missile forces be launched before enemy warheads arrive?

Earlier, we examined a commander's confidence that an attack was under way by using techniques borrowed from Bayesian statistics. The results of this analysis indicated that high levels of confidence (99 percent or more) could be achieved if enough warning messages could be received and validated in the time available. In a worst-case analysis for the Russians, assuming no space-based launch-detection capabilities, the available time could be as short as ten or twelve minutes for an attack by SLBMs. Answers were not found to questions concerning the feasibility due to other problems, such as the time taken by a head of state to order a launch, the impact of current war plans regarding the time of arrival of retaliatory warheads, restricting the number of open silo lids in any given time interval, and the availability, launch readiness, or range limitations of the retaliatory missiles, be they in silos or aboard docked submarines. It was assumed that all SLBMs and ICBMs on either side could be launched on warning for the most effective retaliation. This assumption may be in error, but was made to examine worst-case scenarios. Because of the unknown chance that indications and warning signals might not be forthcoming, or that warning messages might be in error, launch-on-warning tactics could be very dangerous. If there is an error concerning the warning of an attack, one consequence of a rapid retaliation could be societal obliteration. On the other hand, some of our examples indicated that a commander might not have enough confidence that an attack was under way to recommend the prompt launching of all ballistic missiles when some might consider that such a response was appropriate.

In the past the launch-on-warning policy of the United States was unstated, leaving a potential attacker with a huge uncertainty concerning this issue in planning an attack. Under the Clinton administration plans the policy appears to be that the retaliatory forces of the

United States would not be launched on warning. Although Russian capabilities on this score were accidentally tested by the launch of a sounding rocket off the coast of Norway, their continuing persistence in not attempting to launch on warning in the future is highly uncertain. While many observers are worried about the capabilities of the Russian detection systems, the possibility of a Russian launch on warning in response to the sounding-rocket launch arose because of a procedural failure, not an equipment failure. The advance notification of the sounding-rocket launch apparently did not reach the highest levels of the Russian government.

Breaking Out from Future Agreements

Cheating or sudden abrogation of a future arms control agreement could lead to a sudden increase in the number of nuclear warheads deployed by one side. One paramount issue was addressed: the potential damage to U.S. assets if the Russians should break out, assuming that warheads on ICBMs and SLBMs were increased beyond agreed-to payload constraints. At the levels of strategic nuclear-warhead limits considered here (2,500 or 800), a sudden abrogation by Russia could more than double the number of their deployed warheads. This increase in warheads effectively would cause a large increase in potential damage should the Russians undertake a first strike. If the United States were to detect a Russian breakout and deploy more warheads, then the United States would also be able to inflict substantially more damage to Russian valued assets.

The major effect of such a breakout would be a significant change in geopolitical stability. Such a breakout, if it were to occur, would greatly increase the perception of threatening intentions and capabilities, no matter which side decided to break out or cheat. The purpose of future arms control agreements would be to reduce the strategic nuclear threats between the United States and Russia, and to keep new inventory levels low. Avoiding cheating or potential breakout conditions would be a primary goal in negotiating new agreements. Both sides would need to agree to comprehensive verification and confidence-building measures to assure each other that increases in nuclear warheads would be detectable, and that such increases would not be tolerated.

NOTES

1. "Treaty Between the United States of America and the Union of Soviet Socialist Republics on the Reduction and Limitation of Strategic Offensive Arms," *United States Treaties and Other International Agreements*, 31 July 1991. Text available at <www.state.gov>.

2. "Treaty Between the United States of America and the Russian Federation on Further Reduction and Limitation of Strategic Offensive Arms," *United States Treaties and Other International Agreements*, 3 January 1993. Text available at <www.state.gov>.

3. "Joint Statement on Parameters on Future Reductions in Nuclear Forces" (Fact Sheet) (Helsinki: White House Office of the Press Secretary, 21 March 1997).

4. Craig Ciernello, "U.S. and Soviet/Russian Strategic Nuclear Forces," *Arms Control Today* 29, no. 2 (1999): 34; John Deutch, *Nuclear Policy Review* (briefing, 12 September) (Washington, D.C.: U.S. Department of Defense, 1994); Jack Mendelsohn, "START II and Beyond," *Arms Control Today* 26, no. 8 (1996): 3–9; Anton V. Surikov, *Approaches to Mathematical Modeling of the Process of World-Wide Strategic Nuclear Conflict in the Former USSR*, in Melvin L. Best, Jr., John Hughes-Wilson, and Andrei A. Piontkowsky, eds., *Strategic Stability in the Post–Cold War World and the Future of Nuclear Disarmament* (Dordrecht: Kluwer Academic Publishers, 1995), 307 et seq.

5. Robert Linhard, Maj. Gen., USAF, personal communication with the author, March 1993.

6. Stansfield Turner, *Caging the Nuclear Genie* (Boulder, Colo.: Westview Press, 1997); William F. Burns, Chairman, Committee on International Security and Arms Control, *The Future of U.S. Nuclear Weapons Policy* (Washington, D.C.: National Academy Press, 1997).

7. Deutch, *Nuclear Policy Review*; Mendelsohn, *START II*.

8. Surikov, *Approaches*.

9. Bruce Bennett, *Russian Strategic Targets in the Late 1990s*, in *ACDA Future Nuclear Weapons Policy Workshop Final Report*, ed. Steve Bauer and Frank Jenkins (McLean, Va.: Science Applications International Corporation, 1993).

10. Glenn A. Kent and David E. Thaler, *First-Strike Stability: A Methodology for Evaluating Strategic Forces*, R-3765-AF (Santa Monica, Calif.: RAND Corporation, 1989). Glenn A. Kent and David E. Thaler, *First-Strike Stability and Strategic Defenses: Part II of a Methodology for Evaluating Strategic Forces*, R-3918-AF (Santa Monica, Calif.: RAND Corporation, 1990).

11. Salvador B. Layno, "A Model of the ABM–VS–RV Engagement with Imperfect RV Discrimination." *Operations Research* 19 (1971): 1502 et seq.

12. Robert L. Winkler, *An Introduction to Bayesian Inference and Decision* (New York: Holt, Rinehart and Winston, 1972).

13. Robert Jervis, *Perception and Misperception in International Politics* (Princeton, N.J.: Princeton University Press, 1976); Bruce G. Blair, *The Logic of Accidental Nuclear War* (Washington, D.C.: The Brookings Institution, 1993).

14. Thomas C. Schelling, *The Strategy of Conflict* (Cambridge: Harvard University Press, 1960), 230–254.

15. Layno, "A Model of the ABM–VS–RV Engagement."

16. Walter Pincus, "Naval Chief Backs Cut in Force of Trident Subs," *Washington Post*, 7 January 1999, A23.

17. U.S. Naval Institute, *USNI Military Data Base, Global Defense Information*. <www.periscope.ucg.com>.

18. Dick Cheney, *Military Forces in Transition* (Washington, D.C.: U.S. Department of Defense, 1991).

19. David Hoffman, "Russia's Missile Defense Eroding: Gaps in Early-Warning Satellite Coverage Raise Risk of Launch Error," *Washington Post*, 10 February 1999, A1.

20. Bruce G. Blair, Harold A. Feiveson, and Frank von Hippel, "Taking Nuclear Weapons Off Hair-Trigger Alert," *Scientific American* 277, no. 5 (1997): 42–49; Inge Sellevag, *Norwegian Rocket*, <http://web.cs.cmu.edu/afs/cs/usr/dconst/fpspace97/1156.html>, 8 July 1997 (Now out of print).

21. Robert Bell, "Strategic Agreements and the CTB Treaty: Striking the Right Balance," *Arms Control Today* 28, no. 1 (1998).

22. June E. O'Neill, Letter to the Honorable Tom Daschle, U.S. Senate, with attachment (Washington, D.C.: Congressional Budget Office, 3 September 1998). This material is publicly available via <www.cbo.gov>.

5

Proliferation and Pragmatism: Nonproliferation Policy for the Twenty-First Century

William C. Martel

While the end of the twentieth century is marked by numerous successes in foreign policy, unfortunately the same is not true for nonproliferation. Despite the best efforts of the United States and many other countries, we are seeing the end of nonproliferation. Most ominously, India and Pakistan tested nuclear weapons in 1998 and declared their status as nuclear states. Further, Iraq, Iran, and North Korea are actively seeking to develop nuclear weapons and ballistic missiles. Most recently, in October 1999 the United States refused to ratify the Comprehensive Test Ban Treaty. The cumulative effect is a monumental failure of the institutions, regimes, and norms that defined nonproliferation throughout the Cold War.

Fundamentally, U.S. policy advanced the principles that most states do not have legitimate reasons for possessing nuclear weapons, that nuclear proliferation represented a grave threat to U.S. interests, and that adding nuclear powers would increase the chance of nuclear war. Accordingly, the United States sought to limit the number of states to the nuclear signatories of the NPT, notably the United States, the Soviet Union, France, Britain, and, later, China.[1] Furthermore, the United States used international regimes to enforce the ban on the spread of nuclear technologies and materials and the means for delivering such weapons. While this policy was sensible and effective during the Cold War, a number of factors have undermined its effectiveness.

This chapter begins with the argument that U.S. nonproliferation policy is no longer credible. It proceeds to outline a new policy that balances the legitimate aspirations of states that believe nuclear weapons will strengthen their security with the U.S. desire to ensure that unstable or rogue states do not possess nuclear weapons.

FAILURE OF NONPROLIFERATION

By the end of the twentieth century we have seen a failure of nonproliferation policy for several reasons. First and foremost, more states possess nuclear weapons in 2000 than at any time since 1945. While the number of nuclear-weapons states has not risen as fast as some projected in the 1970s, the fact is that there are more nuclear-armed states.[2] In 1993 South Africa announced that it would dismantle its nuclear-weapons program, which it started in 1974.[3] Throughout the 1990s Iraq, Iran, and North Korea have actively sought to develop nuclear-weapons programs.[4] Most recently, in May 1998 India and Pakistan conducted highly public nuclear tests, and by many accounts are "weaponizing" their nuclear devices.[5] These nuclear programs are expensive, often costing in the realm of $10 to 20 billion. And these states often receive technical support from the major nuclear powers, most notably China.[6]

Second, it is increasingly difficult for the United States to persuade states to refrain from developing nuclear weapons. The threat that the United States or the international community will impose political and economic sanctions is not terribly effective and has been largely ignored. For instance, despite strong pressure from the United States and the United Nations that they would impose sanctions, Pakistan was not dissuaded from testing nuclear weapons.[7] Similarly, despite the threat of sanctions, Iran, Iraq, North Korea, Pakistan, India, Israel, and South Africa have either developed nuclear weapons or are actively seeking to do so.

Third, the international mechanisms for controlling the spread of nuclear-weapons technologies have not prevented the diffusion of nuclear knowledge. The failure of export controls and nuclear regulatory regimes, such as the NPT and the International Atomic Energy Agency (IAEA), are legendary.[8] Iraq was developing nuclear weapons while it was under inspection by the IAEA, and North Korea pursued its weapons-development program while a signatory to the NPT.[9] Despite persistent reports of an active Iranian nuclear weapons program, the IAEA dismissed reports about that program after inspections.[10] One consequence of these events is that the Cold War mechanisms for controlling access to nuclear technologies and materials have not prevented states from developing nuclear weapons.

States Want Nuclear Weapons

Despite these policies and mechanisms, states apparently believe that nuclear weapons are critical to defending their interests. This logic has always applied to nuclear proliferation. The fundamental principle is that national leaderships believe that nuclear weapons improve a state's security. The history of the Cold War reinforces this conclusion insofar as the possession of nuclear weapons contributed to the security of the United States, the Soviet Union, China, and Western European states during the Cold War. By imposing enormous costs on potential aggressors and increasing one's freedom of maneuver against nonnuclear states, nuclear weapons make the costs of war too great to bear.[11]

When a state's leadership makes the decision to possess nuclear weapons, it does so after a careful and prudent analysis of the complex security tradeoffs, which include the risk of preemptive attacks, regional hostility, and war. While states that possess nuclear weapons are acutely aware of the hostile reactions that their decision will provoke, a significant number of states have opted for nuclear weapons.

At the same time, each state is uniquely qualified to judge its own security interests, the ability of other states to interfere with its interests, and its ability to defend the state's interests. This logic runs contrary to nonproliferation policy, which historically implied that foreign observers can properly judge whether other states should possess nuclear weapons. The failure of nonproliferation is partially related to the belief that possessing nuclear weapons is a prudent way to defend one's interests, and is not an example of a failure in strategic thinking.

RETHINKING NUCLEAR PROLIFERATION

The problem is that for decades the United States rejected each of these nonproliferation propositions. Instead, U.S. policy promoted the ideas that nuclear weapons undermine security, that possessing nuclear weapons is a case of flawed strategic thinking, and that the United States is best positioned to judge which states, if any, should possess nuclear weapons. But since the cumulative events of the 1990s caused nonproliferation policy to collapse of its own weight, it is time to rethink the principles on which U.S. nuclear nonproliferation policy rests.

U.S. Power to Control Proliferation Is Limited

A characteristic of the twenty-first century is that the United States and the international community will not be able to persuade states that developing nuclear weapons harms their national interests. The problem is complicated by the fact that many states possess the scientific, technological, and economic resources that are necessary for developing nuclear weapons. The Iraqi case is interesting because it demonstrates that, despite the best efforts of the international community, a state with sufficient determination and wealth can assemble the technological complex for developing nuclear weapons.[12] The Indian and Pakistani examples are noteworthy because these states demonstrated that the West's nonproliferation rhetoric was not matched by its willingness to use and enforce political, economic, and military sanctions.

One reason for the failure of nonproliferation policy is technological. Nuclear weapons have existed for more than fifty years, which means that states can find the requisite scientific and technical talent to assemble nuclear weapons. And with the collapse of the former Soviet Union, states may be able to gain access to fissile materials, scientists, and possibly nuclear weapons. As a result, it is relatively easy for states to circumvent the controls that were established by the NPT to control the fissile materials that are produced by civilian nuclear facilities.[13] For example, both Iraq and South Africa produced fissile materials in civilian research reactors that had not been declared to the IAEA.

States Value Nuclear Weapons

There is an overwhelming empirical record that many states, most notably India and Pakistan, believe that nuclear weapons increase their security. While the conclusion that nuclear weapons strengthened security is consistent with the experiences of the United States, the Soviet Union, China, and their respective allies, the United States adheres to the dogma that nuclear weapons should be possessed only by the states that are permanent members of the U.N. Security Council, or our close allies, such as Great Britain and Israel. Nonproliferation rhetoric aside, the underlying principle is that most states cannot be trusted to behave responsibly with nuclear weapons.

At its core, nonproliferation policy is discriminatory because it divides the world into nuclear "haves" and "have-nots" on the basis of imprecise and unstated criteria, and specifies which states are entitled to possess nuclear weapons. This discriminatory policy entails significant political costs, as exemplified by the poor state of U.S.–Pakistani relations, which have been dominated by the U.S. condemnation of Pakistan for its nuclear program.[14]

The ideal toward which U.S. policy should strive is that nuclear weapons contribute to security, but we live in a time when nuclear weapons are less important. If the United States and other states want to reduce the importance of nuclear weapons, then our policy must limit the nonproliferation rhetoric. The danger is that the fixation in

U.S. nonproliferation policy on preventing the spread of nuclear weapons strengthens the argument of those who assert that they need nuclear weapons to counterbalance U.S. power. This was reaffirmed when the Indian Army chief of staff, General K. Sundarji, observed, "The lesson of Desert Storm is don't mess with the United States without nuclear weapons." The more the nuclear states say about nuclear weapons, the more states are likely to conclude that they should possess them.

Emphasize Stable Cases of Proliferation

While the United States has historically declared that all cases of nuclear proliferation undermine international security, the twenty-first century provides an opportunity to consider the concept that nuclear proliferation can strengthen international security. The decisions by Israel, India, Pakistan, and South Africa (albeit temporarily) to join the nuclear club did not diminish international security, and in the case of South Asia helped to deter war and shape a potentially stable nuclear balance of power between New Delhi and Islamabad. Even in the earlier years of their emerging nuclear relationship, Indian and Pakistani nuclear capabilities probably helped to avert a war during the Kashmir crisis in the spring of 1990.[15] Nevertheless, these states faced the age-old problem of deterrence: Nuclear weapons limit their options and thereby dissuade states from using them.

If nuclear weapons inhibit states from taking military action, then proliferation can have stabilizing effects. In that case, the United States should reconsider the principle that all cases of nuclear proliferation create instability and therefore jeopardize U.S. interests. However, the argument that nuclear proliferation could enhance stability is a form of heresy for the nonproliferation community. If the United States defines a new nonproliferation policy that changes the prevailing beliefs about nuclear proliferation, it must begin with outlining what stability means in a world that is occupied by ten or twenty rather than five or six nuclear states. Despite the failure of nonproliferation, the operant assumption behind governmental policy and international regimes is that the fear of instability will lead states to refrain from acquiring nuclear weapons. If some cases of proliferation can have stabilizing effects, the United States should institutionalize policies that encourage nuclear states to abide by the rules of deterrent stability.[16]

The implication is that the international regimes used for controlling proliferation are necessarily obsolete. To preserve the credibility of institutions such as the IAEA, we must define nonproliferation objectives that are consistent with their capabilities. The United States is uniquely positioned to advocate a reorganization of these institutions, many of which are relics of now-unenforceable restrictions on nuclear ownership.

The first step for the United States is to define why nuclear proliferation is not necessarily destabilizing. This new policy should combine the idea that not all nuclear states will contribute to instability with the principle that it is prudent for the United States to help nuclear states build safe and secure arsenals.

Nuclear-Free States Can Be Major Powers

In theory, a significant step to changing the prevailing perceptions about proliferation would be to recognize that a state's status as major power is not defined by the possession of nuclear weapons. While nuclear weapons obviously add to a state's military power, security, and status, it is equally true that nuclear-free states can be major powers in their own right. To move beyond the current nonproliferation policy, the United States should create an environment in which states that choose to forego nuclear weapons are viewed as major powers, as exemplified by the case of Germany and Japan.

One of the unintended consequences of seeking to prevent nuclear proliferation has been to enhance the value of nuclear weapons. The reason is that when the international community engages in protracted policy debates about the need to dissuade Pakistan or India from developing nuclear weapons it implicitly reinforces the point that nuclear weapons are very important. And if nuclear weapons were not significant, then states logically would not waste the time or political capital on policies that seek to persuade others to remain nonnuclear. The very tone and content of nonproliferation policy reaffirms that nuclear weapons have immense political and strategic significance. As examples, consider the attention that was devoted to North Korea, Iraq, Pakistan, and India during the last decade.

The ideal toward which the United States should strive is to shape the attitude that major-power status is not derived from nuclear ownership. Germany and Japan are members of the Group of Eight industrial nations, have immense political and economic power and influence, and clearly could produce nuclear weapons, but have deliberately chosen not to do so—in part because the U.S. nuclear umbrella protects them, and because nuclear weapons would become a sensitive political problem. One concrete way to build the perception that non-nuclear states can be major powers would be to put nonweapon states on the permanent membership of the U.N. Security Council and thus demonstrate that nuclear status is not the sine qua non of permanent membership on the Security Council.

FOUR PRINCIPLES OF U.S. PROLIFERATION POLICY

Once we accept the proposition that nuclear proliferation has proceeded despite the active resistance of the international community, it is time to shape nonproliferation policies that promote peace and stability. Such a policy would rest on four principles.

First, nuclear ownership by any state is an open issue, contingent upon behavior that conforms to international standards. While during the Cold War the United States saw all cases of nuclear proliferation as destabilizing, it is time to judge each case of nuclear ownership on its merits and with an open mind. From this principle it follows that the United States is not inherently opposed to all cases of nuclear proliferation, and that nuclear proliferation is not inherently destabilizing or contrary to our interests. This is a radical departure from the past.

In theory, it is difficult to demonstrate that nuclear-armed states will be compelled to follow the accepted standards of international behavior. However, if a state abides by the norms of stabilizing behavior, the United States must be prepared to accept its nuclear ownership. This policy is not intended to mask the unstated preference for a world in which only a few states, including the United States, possess nuclear weapons, because whether we approve or not, the United States cannot preserve the nuclear status quo indefinitely. As long as nuclear weapons remain a fixture of international politics, the pragmatic policy is to make nuclear ownership as consistent with peace and security as possible.

Second, the United States seeks to reduce the incentives that drive states toward nuclear ownership. Nuclear ownership does not occur in a political or strategic vacuum, but exists because the state's leadership believes that nuclear weapons will enhance their security. An important first step is to reduce the incentives that drive states toward nuclear ownership, but the problem is that U.S. policy has focused on the disincentives to possessing nuclear weapons, of which the most prominent is the threat of political and economic isolation. In the case of North Korea the United States offered security guarantees if Pyongyang terminated its nuclear-weapons program, but this policy ultimately rested on the threat of economic sanctions and military intervention.[17] It is no longer credible to base our policy on the threat that the costs of nuclear ownership will be more burdensome than states can bear. States have willingly taken this risk, and it is likely that other states may conclude that the cost of nuclear ownership is worthwhile.

U.S. nonproliferation policy must shift to using incentives to change the perception that nuclear weapons fundamentally determine whether a state is a great power, and that nuclear weapons are the central measure of power. Several quite simple steps, including elevating Germany and Japan to the ranks of permanent members of the U.N. Security Council, would demonstrate that nuclear ownership is not a prerequisite of great power status, and that economic power can be an equally important measure of great power.

This policy can use unilateral and multilateral security guarantees to lessen the value of nuclear ownership. For example, during the Cold War the United States extended security guarantees to many states in order to reduce their incentive to possess their own nuclear deterrent. To this day, a measure of this policy's success is that Germany and Japan remain nonnuclear states. In theory, U.S. nonproliferation policy could use positive incentives rather than denunciations to persuade states that nuclear weapons will not necessarily solve their security concerns.

Third, the United States will use political, economic, and military measures to avert nuclear ownership by states that manifest destabilizing behavior. While the United States historically sought to slow or prevent virtually all cases of nuclear proliferation, future U.S. policy must concentrate on preventing those cases of proliferation in which a state may behave in a destabilizing fashion. This means that the United States would oppose a state's nuclear program based on its behavior, and not simply because we are opposed to all cases of proliferation. When an instance of nuclear ownership will strengthen regional peace and security, the United States should not actively oppose that program. That being said, when the United States judges that nuclear weapons in the hands of a state will have potentially destabilizing consequences, it should employ the full range of political, economic, and military instruments that we used during the Cold War to avert the spread of nuclear weapons. This policy would rely on the traditional nonproliferation mechanisms that we used during the Cold War era, including national and international regimes for controlling nuclear materials, export control mechanisms, and punitive political, economic, and military sanctions. Most of the existing governmental mechanisms are well suited for supporting this policy.

This policy will place pressure on the United States to take action rather than simply use rhetoric to condemn the state. If we are to reaffirm the principle that states that manifest destabilizing behavior will not be permitted to possess nuclear weapons, then the United States must be willing to take significant steps to resist destabilizing cases of nuclear proliferation.

By its nature, this policy is less discriminatory because it carefully evaluates the risks of nuclear ownership in each case, rather than automatically opposing all cases of nuclear ownership. With this policy, states would be perfectly free to seek to possess nuclear weapons, and would not be discouraged from doing so, provided that their pattern of behavior conforms with internationally accepted standards. Naturally, it would be highly prudent for the United States to discourage states that have supported international terrorism or fomented instability from acquiring nuclear weapons. When the United States confronts cases in which a state's behavior raises these concerns, Washington should use either unilateral or multilateral measures to avert nuclear ownership, or if necessary eliminate those weapons with military force. While it is unlikely that this policy would persuade rogue states to cease their nuclear programs or change their behavior, this policy would narrow the growing gap between the rhetoric and practice of U.S. nonproliferation policy, and thereby ensure that our nonproliferation policies are credible.

Fourth, the U.S. nonproliferation policy places the emphasis on security and safety. It is essential for states that want to possess nuclear weapons to develop the policies and practices that enable them to maintain their nuclear forces in a safe and secure fashion. Based on its fifty years of expertise, the United States has the technical and operational experience to help the new nuclear states develop appropriate mechanisms and institutions that are consistent with nuclear stability. This policy would allow the United States to help Russia dismantle its nuclear arsenal and employ nuclear scientists, as well as help Pakistan and India develop secure and reliable command and control systems.

A prominent lesson of the nuclear age is that secure command and control systems enhance stability.[18] Neither the international community nor that state can be confident that its nuclear forces are safe and secure if there are no established lines of authority between political and military echelons, or if there is no tradition in which the military is subordinate to political authorities. It is virtually certain that it will take decades before most nuclear states will have the expertise and technology that is needed to ensure that nuclear forces are kept under tight political and operational control. The safeguards that kept U.S. forces secure for decades must be available so that all nuclear states can establish the mechanisms and procedures for ensuring tight control over nuclear forces. Safe and secure nuclear forces are essential for global stability in a multinuclear world, and the United States can help these states maintain their nuclear forces in ways that enhance rather than undermine security.

NONPROLIFERATION POLICY FOR THE TWENTY-FIRST CENTURY

As this chapter suggests, it is imperative for the United States to establish a new policy before the uncontrolled process of nuclear proliferation leads to the complete erosion of the credibility of nonproliferation efforts. There are several steps that would help the United States realign the rhetoric and substance of its nonproliferation policy.

Reject Dual Standards of Nuclear Ownership

The intellectual foundation for nonproliferation policy during the Cold War, as enshrined in the NPT, was to divide the world into nuclear "haves" and "have-nots." Not surprisingly, the developing states argued that this dual standard of nuclear ownership was discriminatory and unjust because it declared that only certain states should possess nuclear weapons. The actions of India, Iraq, Iran, North Korea, and Pakistan have all shown that they reject this principle.[19] Now that nuclear weapons are no longer the revolutionary weapon that they were during the Cold War, it is futile to promote policies that depend on dual standards of nuclear ownership.

Strengthen Stabilizing Cases

This nonproliferation policy will succeed if the United States can support states that show a willingness to manage their nuclear weapons in a stabilizing fashion. If, for example, Pakistan's nuclear arsenal effectively deters Indian aggression, and India's nuclear arsenal has the same deterrent effect on Pakistan, then we may conclude that nuclear weapons have stabilizing characteristics. When states are locked in a permanent "nuclear embrace," they are compelled to live with the same constraints on their behavior that applied, with considerable success, to the United States and Soviet Union during the Cold War.

Once the United States recognizes that there may be stabilizing cases of nuclear proliferation, U.S. nonproliferation policy will be more credible and effective. If, arguably, nuclear weapons stabilized the U.S.–Soviet relationship and averted a major war in Europe, then in theory nuclear weapons could have the same positive effect on the next generation of nuclear powers. It is time for governments and societies to discuss the essential conditions for nuclear stability in a world in which we cannot control which states possess weapons of mass destruction. Now is the time to recognize the long-overdue revolution in the way that governments and societies think about the effects of nuclear proliferation on regional stability.

Aggressively Prevent Destabilizing Proliferation

What will never change is that nuclear weapons in the hands of some states could be so profoundly destabilizing that the United States would be forced to take political, economic, and military action. Three contemporary examples of destabilizing proliferation highlight the problems the United States will face.

First, Iran's apparent decision to become a nuclear-weapons power will have profound destabilizing consequences for the Middle East.[20] The prospect of a nuclear-armed Iran will provoke reactions that range from preemptive attacks by states such as Israel that fear Iran will use nuclear weapons for dangerous purposes. A second case is a North Korean nuclear program, which could cause a conventional war to spread from the Korean peninsula to Japan and other Asian states. Nuclear weapons would lock North Korea into a deterrent relationship with the United States, and in the event of a reunified Korea could create instability in Northeast Asia.

A third danger is that terrorist organizations will seek to acquire nuclear weapons, or that states will provide support for terrorist organizations, which is one reason why the Iranian and North Korean nuclear programs are seen as so destabilizing. While it has been unlikely that terrorist organizations would possess nuclear weapons, we cannot dismiss the possibility that substate groups might acquire nuclear weapons. The fear has been that the breakup of the former Soviet Union's nuclear complex will make nuclear weapons and materials more available to rogue states and organizations. While it is highly unlikely that nuclear weapons will be developed in a terrorist workshop or that terrorist organizations could develop "suitcase bombs," U.S. nonproliferation policy must anticipate that some states might provide weapons and technology to terrorist organizations. In its present economic condition, North Korea is especially dangerous, because its economic collapse creates powerful incentives to exchange nuclear weapons or technology for hard currency or energy resources.

As the United States uses a combination of diplomatic tools and military intervention to prevent destabilizing cases of nuclear proliferation, we should understand that there is no substitute for having the political will to act early before a state develops nuclear weapons. And even if states are willing to act aggressively, we should recall that it took a major theater war to halt the development of Iraq's nuclear program.

Reduce Value of Nuclear Weapons

The United States should work to demonstrate that nuclear weapons are no longer the currency of international power and prestige, and to diminish the incentives that motivate states to possess nuclear weapons. When states realize that nuclear weapons do not generate opportunities for extracting political and economic concessions from the international community, in theory nuclear weapons should have less political and military appeal. If the United States and the international community downplay the role of nuclear weapons, we will reduce the ability of states to use these weapons for political and diplomatic leverage.

The current approach, however, suggests that nuclear weapons are a critical determinant of power and prestige. Events in North Korea, Pakistan, Iran, and Iraq suggest that leaders believe nuclear weapons are important, and that until nuclear weapons are seen as less important it will be difficult to persuade leaders that these weapons are not a fundamental measure of power. Leaders generally understand that nuclear weapons give them the ability to command a prominent place in U.S. foreign policy. The United States can diminish the value of nuclear weapons by linking our political and economic support to a state's decision that it will not develop or acquire these weapons. This was the policy of linkage that the United States used when it tied economic assistance to Ukraine in exchange for Kiev's decision to relinquish its nuclear weapons.[21] A second approach is to use bilateral and multilateral security guarantees or assurances to demonstrate that states have means other than nuclear weapons for protecting their interests.

A third approach is to develop defensive systems so that the United States can protect itself, its allies, and its overseas military forces. The ability to defend oneself against a nuclear attack will reduce the military effectiveness of nuclear weapons, and perhaps persuade states that nuclear weapons cannot be effectively delivered on target, are vulnerable to preemptive attack by smart conventional munitions or nuclear weapons, and are therefore not effective instruments of national power. A comprehensive policy on nuclear nonproliferation should use a combination of defensive weapons and intelligence systems to reduce the military effectiveness and political power associated with nuclear weapons.

CONCLUSIONS

During the Cold War states learned that there are legitimate reasons, as outlined in classical deterrence theory, for acquiring nuclear weapons.[22] While the United States historically has sought to discourage states from possessing nuclear weapons, we need a more effective policy for the twenty-first century to reverse the tendency among many leaders to believe that they should develop nuclear weapons. U.S. nonproliferation policy has been weakened by our failure to persuade states that they do not need nuclear weapons. While in an ideal world it might be preferable to abolish nuclear weapons or to entrust those weapons to a small number of states, neither condition is ever likely to exist.

Another reason for the failure of U.S. policy is that our stalwart opposition to proliferation has effectively destroyed our ability to influence the nuclear-armed states in precisely those cases where coopera-tion is the most urgent. No example better illustrates this dilemma than the fact that U.S. relations with India and Pakistan are held hostage to the impasse over the U.S. condemnation of their nuclear weapons.

For the reasons outlined in this chapter, the end of the twentieth century coincides with the end of nonproliferation. We need a new nonproliferation policy for the twenty-first century that is based on selective rather than universal opposition to nuclear proliferation, helps the new nuclear states acquire the technologies that create reliable com-mand and control systems, discourages the first use of nuclear weap-ons, and helps these states manage their nuclear arsenals in safe and secure ways. Most fundamentally, U.S. policy should move beyond the declarations that states should not acquire nuclear weapons or that the United States will base its policy on judging whether states should "go nuclear," to constructive policies that seek to build security among nuclear states.

There is no argument that U.S. nonproliferation policy was success-ful during the Cold War. While the reasons are complex, perhaps in-cluding our attachment to the ideology of nonproliferation, U.S. nonproliferation policy is failing because it remains committed to prin-ciples that were enunciated at the depths of the Cold War. If U.S. policy is not consistent with contemporary strategic circumstances, we will witness the end of nonproliferation and the emergence of a time when states routinely believe that nuclear weapons are the best answer to security. By distinguishing between stabilizing and destabilizing pro-liferation, the United States can help nuclear-armed states coexist peacefully. The United States can no longer afford to waste its cred-ibility on proliferation cases that do not threaten our vital interests, and must focus our diplomatic machinery on the most dangerous cases.

In conclusion, U.S. nonproliferation policy must employ a careful blend of positive and negative sanctions to persuade states that nuclear weapons are not the answer to their security problems. But to succeed the United States must have the political will to act politically, eco-nomically, and militarily to prevent the proliferation of nuclear weap-ons to states that violate standards of acceptable international behavior. If the international community relies on the old policy, we will lose our ability to convince states that nuclear weapons are not the instru-ment of choice for defending their interests.

NOTES

1. China, which is not an original signatory to the NPT, only agreed to adhere to the terms of the treaty in 1992.

2. See Thomas W. Graham, "Winning the Nonproliferation Battle," *Arms Control Today* 21, no. 7 (1991): 8–13, for a discussion of these nuclear programs.

3. See J. W. de Villiers, Roger Jardine, and Mitchell Reiss, "Why South Africa Gave Up the Bomb," *Foreign Affairs* 72 (1993): 98–109.

4. In the case of North Korea, David Kay described the North Korean case as one "where nonproliferation has failed." See Andrew Weinschenk, "North Korea's Actions Bring Protest Storm from Officials," *Defense Week*, 8 November 1993, 3.

5. "Asia's Nuclear Coming of Age," *BBC News*, 1 June 1998; "Pakistan, Answering India, Carries Out Nuclear Tests," *New York Times*, 29 May 1998, A1. See also "A New Threat in South Asia," *Newsweek*, 18 October 1999; "Thinking the Unthinkable: Nuclear War in South Asia," *Associated Press*, 31 May 1998. More recent information on the output of nuclear reactors in India and Pakistan suggests that India could produce roughly 450 weapons and Pakistan upward of 100 weapons. See "Report: India, Pakistan Can Make More Nuclear Weapons Than Thought," *CNN*, 23 September 1998. For more conservative estimates, which placed the size of the Indian and Pakistani nuclear arsenals at eighty-six and thirty-six weapons, respectively, by the year 2000, see "Pakistan's Nuclear Punch," *ABC News/Reuters*, 14 May 1998. For background on the Chinese, British, and French nuclear arsenals, see *Military Balance* (Oxford: Oxford University Press for the IISS, 1998).

6. See David Albright and Mark Hibbs, "Iraq's Bomb: Blueprints and Artifacts," *Bulletin of Atomic Scientists* 48, no. 1 (1992): 31–40. "India's Choice, and Pakistan's," *New York Times*, 29 May 1998, A19 ("China has been transferring nuclear-warhead blueprints to Islamabad since about 1980"). Also, "The US Central Intelligence Agency (CIA)'s annual report to Congress in 1997 states that 'China has provided extensive support to Pakistan's WMD capabilities.'" See Brahma Chellaney, "After the Tests: India's Options," *Survival* 40, no. 4 (1998–1999): 100–101.

7. The United States will attempt to delay future loans from the World Bank, the International Monetary Fund, and private U.S. banks to Pakistan. For details on the sanctions imposed against India and Pakistan, see the testimony of Ambassador David L. Aaron, Undersecretary of Commerce for International Trade, on the implementation of India–Pakistan economic sanctions in House International Relations Subcommittee, 105th Congress, *Hearings on India–Pakistan Nuclear Proliferation*, 18 June 1998, pp. 1–3. For a review of the reactions of the major states, which ranged from expressions of concern to withdrawals of economic aid, see "Aid Cuts, Strong Words," *ABC News*, 28 May 1998.

8. The argument that the NPT is broken is itself contentious. For the views that it is broken, see "It's Broke, So Fix It: The Nuclear Nonproliferation Treaty Is in Urgent Need of Repair," *The Economist*, 27 July 1991, 13; Ashok Kapur, "Dump the Treaty," *Bulletin of the Atomic Scientists* 46, no. 6 (1990): 21–23. For the contrary view, see Lewis A. Dunn, "It Ain't Broke—Don't Fix It," *Bulletin of the Atomic Scientists* 46, no. 6 (1990): 19–21. See Ann Marie Cunningham, "Wanted: An Astute Nuclear Detective," *Technology Review*, October 1993, 13, for criticisms about the IAEA's performance. The alternative view is that the flaws in the IAEA safeguards system have been repaired, and the United States should increase its support for the IAEA. See Robert L. Gallucci, "Nuclear

Situation in Iraq," *U.S. Department of State Dispatch*, 5 July 1993, 483.

9. See Cunningham, "Wanted: An Astute Nuclear Detective," 13, for criticisms about the IAEA's contradictory goals of promoting nuclear energy and preventing nuclear proliferation.

10. See "U.N. Reports on A-Arms Threat," *Facts on File*, 5 March 1992, 157.

11. For American diplomacy, deterrence was the operational embodiment of the judgment that it was necessary to contain the Soviet Union and communism without permitting our political differences to escalate into a nuclear war. We can trace this principle in the dominant writings on deterrence of which the following is a selection of the more important works on the role of nuclear weapons and deterrence in contemporary international relations: Bernard Brodie, *Strategy in the Missile Age* (Princeton, N.J.: Princeton University Press, 1959); Herman Kahn, *On Thermonuclear War* (Princeton, N.J.: Princeton University Press, 1961); Alexander L. George and Richard Smoke, *Deterrence in American Foreign Policy: Theory and Practice* (New York: Columbia University Press, 1974); Philip Green, *Deadly Logic* (Columbus: Ohio State University, 1966); Morton Halperin and Thomas Schelling, *Strategy and Arms Control* (New York: Twentieth Century Fund, 1961); Henry A. Kissinger, *Nuclear Weapons and Foreign Policy* (New York: Harper & Row, 1957); Thomas C. Schelling, *Arms and Influence* (New Haven: Yale University Press, 1966).

12. While I disagree, a careful account of the argument that the essential logic of nonproliferation remains unchanged is presented in Graham, "Winning the Nonproliferation Battle."

13. See Kurt M. Campbell et al., *Soviet Nuclear Fission: Control of the Nuclear Arsenal in a Disintegrating Soviet Union*, CSIA Studies in International Security no. 1 (Cambridge: Harvard University Press, 1991), for a detailed examination of the problems associated with the fragmentation of the nuclear arsenal in the former Soviet Union.

14. "Wealthy Nations Cut Aid to Pakistan Over Nuclear Tests, *New York Times*, 29 May 1998, A8; "Sanctions Could Bruise Fragile Pakistan Badly," *New York Times*, 29 May 1998, A7.

15. See Seymour M. Hersh, "On the Nuclear Edge," *New Yorker*, 29 March 1993, 56–73, for a detailed review of the role of nuclear weapons in the 1990 Kashmir crisis, and the mutual agreement not to escalate future crises by preemptive strikes against the other's nuclear facilities.

16. Peter D. Feaver, "Command and Control in Emerging Nuclear Nations," *International Security* 17, no. 3 (1992–1993): 160–187.

17. See Carol J. Williams, "N. Korea Agrees to Inspection of 7 Nuclear Sites," *Los Angeles Times*, 16 February 1994, 1; David E. Danger, "North Koreans Agree to Survey of Atomic Sites," *New York Times*, 16 February 1994, A1. Possible answers to North Korea's reversal include fears of economic sanctions, efforts to gain time for the diversion of more plutonium to nuclear weapons, and fears of U.S. military options.

18. Feaver, "Command and Control."

19. The more general view is that it is acceptable for some states—notably the original nuclear-weapons states as enshrined in the NPT—to possess nuclear weapons. However, this view does not sidestep the inherently discriminatory nature of nonproliferation policies.

20. See Michael Eisenstadt, "Living With a Nuclear Iran," *Survival*, Autumn 1999, 124–148.

21. William C. Martel, "Is Ukraine a Universal Example of Nonproliferation?" *Defense Analysis*, December 1998, pp. 198–212.

22. This included countering a rival's nuclear weapons, deterring attacks on the homeland, balancing an opponent's conventional advantages, using nuclear weapons as a far cheaper option than conventional forces, and strengthening the state's prestige and legitimacy.

6

Triage of Triads: Does the United States Really Need Three Strategic-Retaliatory Forces?

Stephen J. Cimbala

Despite nonhostile political relations between the United States and Russia since 1991, the stability of the balance between those two leading nuclear powers is still the subject of considerable political interest and bilateral arms control. In addition, the costs of national defense and military preparedness, including the costs of nuclear modernization and arms reductions, are matters of concern to both Russian and American national leaderships. Finally, both U.S. and Russian decisions about their nuclear-arms buildups or builddowns send signals to nonnuclear states with regard to the probable significance of nuclear weapons in the new world order.

This chapter considers various U.S. options for strategic nuclear forces consistent with the expected requirements of START III, already negotiated in principle between the U.S. and Russian national leaderships. First, we compare four possible models of START III compliant U.S. forces in order to assess their relative operational performances. Second, we consider other attributes of these forces related to the problem of crisis stability. Third, we discuss the problem of defenses against nuclear attack and potential significance for U.S.–Russian nuclear-arms reductions.

WHY NUCLEAR WEAPONS STILL MATTER

Contrary to some expectations, nuclear weapons and arms control issues have not vanished over the horizon in a post–Desert Storm euphoria. There are at least six reasons for this.

First, Russia still has many thousands of nuclear weapons, including those of intercontinental range. Second, the other acknowledged nuclear powers, in addition to the United States and Russia, show no inclination to abandon nuclear weapons as ultimate deterrents. China is, in fact, by all accounts engaged in a significant modernization of its military technology base, including the base that supports improved delivery systems for nuclear weapons. A third reason for the continued importance of nuclear deterrence is the addition of India and Pakistan in 1998 to the club of acknowledged nuclear powers, and the potential for additional nonnuclear states to acquire these and other weapons of mass destruction. Fourth, nuclear deterrence remains important because nonstate actors, including terrorists, interstate criminal organizations (ICOs), and revolutionary actors of various sorts may acquire nuclear or other weapons of mass destruction. Although for some of their purposes nuclear weapons would be superfluous, for other objectives they would, even in small numbers and of puny yields, be quite appropriate. Terrorists who could present a plausible threat to detonate even a small nuclear device within a target state could raise the potential risk of hostage-rescue operations, for hostages and for armed forces of the target state.[1] Terrorists allied with a state actor and equipped with nuclear weapons could gain valuable intelligence, sanctuary, and diplomatic cover from their ally.

A fifth reason for the continuing significance of nuclear deterrence in the post–Cold War system is, somewhat paradoxically, Russia's military and economic weakness. There are two aspects of this weakness that might contribute to nuclear deterrence failure based on failed crisis management, mistaken preemption, or accidental or inadvertent war. First, Russia's conventional military weakness makes it more reliant on nuclear weapons as weapons of first choice or first use, instead of last resort.[2] Second, Russia's economic problems mean that it will have difficulty maintaining personnel morale and reliability. In addition, Russia's military will also be lacking in funds to modernize and properly equip its early warning and nuclear command, control, and communications systems. These weaknesses may encourage reliance on prompt launch doctrines for strategic nuclear retaliation, or raise the odds in favor of a mistaken decision for preemption.

Sixth, Russia's new draft military doctrine of October 1999 reaffirmed the significance of nuclear weapons in Russian military strategy by noting that nuclear arms are an "effective factor of deterrence, guaranteeing the military security of the Russian Federation and its allies, supporting international stability and peace."[3] And despite the dire financial straits in which Russia's conventional military forces found themselves at century's end, civilian and military leaders reaffirmed the priority of nuclear-force modernization in the face of NATO enlargement and possible U.S. deployments of ballistic missile defenses.[4]

The draft military doctrine of 1999 was less significant for its military–technical aspects than for its political frame of reference. Compared to its 1993 predecessor, it was explicitly anti-Western and anti-United States. Expressing the Kremlin's obvious pique at having to swallow NATO enlargement and Operation Allied Force against Yugoslavia in 1999, the draft doctrine contrasted two opposed trends. The first trend was unipolar, meaning U.S. superpower domination; the second, multipolar, including many centers of influence, including Russia.[5] Nuclear weapons guarantee Russia a seat at the great power table and, thus, a claim to future status as one of the influential poles in a twenty-first century-multipolar international system.

FORCE STRUCTURES AND ARMS CONTROL

It was an accepted truism during most of the Cold War that U.S. strategic nuclear forces had to be distributed among three kinds of delivery systems: land-based ballistic missiles, submarine-launched ballistic missiles, and a variety of weapons delivered by bombers of intercontinental range, including gravity bombs, short-range attack missiles (SRAMs), and air-launched cruise missiles (ALCMs) (SRAMs are no longer in the U.S. inventory; today's bomber force carries gravity bombs and ALCMs). In addition to ALCMs, nuclear-armed cruise missiles could also be launched from surface ships or submarines (SLCMs; sea launched cruise missiles). Air- and sea-launched cruise missiles also can be tasked for conventional missions, as they were during the Gulf War of 1991 and against Yugoslavia in 1999.

The strategic rationales for this triad of forces were of three kinds.[6] First, by distributing retaliatory forces across three kinds of launchers, the United States could complicate the plans of any attacker. A first striker would have to attack the various U.S. land-based, sea-based, and air-delivery systems in different ways. On account of this first factor, the attacker's plans would be confounded by necessary and undesirable trade-offs. For example, an attacker might have to choose between simultaneous or sequential launches of its ICBMs and SLBMs. If land- and sea-based missiles were launched simultaneously against U.S. targets, the early arriving SLBMs would provide additional warning time for American ICBMs to escape destruction via prompt launch. On the other hand, if attacking ICBMs and SLBMs were launched sequentially in order to destroy more of the American land-based missile force, then additional time would be available to scramble U.S. bombers out from under the attack.

A second argument for the triad was that each leg created a different problem for any missile or air defenses deployed by the other side. Having bombers and two types of missiles meant that even highly competent ballistic missile defenses could not obviate destruction from air-delivered weapons. For the same reason, air defenses were of no value against attacking missiles. A third aspect of the triad touted by its defenders was the avoidance of vulnerability due to any single technology breakthrough. If, for example, the United States were to reduce its offensive retaliatory forces to a monad based on submarines as some have advocated, then a singular breakthrough in antisubmarine warfare technology would negate the U.S. deterrent (it should be noted that current or foreseeable technology offers no such possibility).

These strategic rationales were supported by strong forces in domestic politics. Each military service wanted a piece of the action of strategic nuclear warfare. The navy's sea-based ballistic missile force was a complement to the air force's Strategic Air Command. The air force and the army contested for at least a decade the issue of who would control land-based missiles. After many battles a truce of sorts allotted the mission of offensive retaliation by means of land-based ballistic missiles to the air force. The army acquired ballistic missile defense as its turf. These decisions about roles and missions, reached during the latter 1950s and early 1960s, have largely carried forward to the present day. Modernization of nuclear forces and research and development on potential antinuclear defenses (from Project Defender through the present Clinton version of limited defenses against accidental launches or rogue attacks) has continued to distribute the domestic economic spillovers of weapons procurement and deployment across the various services and across many Congressional districts as well.

The end of the Cold War and the demise of the Soviet Union have led to an acknowledgment by virtually all observers that American and Russian nuclear weapons could be greatly reduced in number. The United States and Russia signed START II in 1993 (finally ratified by Russian in 2000), which requires that each state reduce the number of its accountable warheads on long-range delivery systems to 3,000 to 3,500. Both the Clinton and Putin administrations have discussed further reductions under a START III regime that would reduce both sides' accountable forces to some 2,000 to 2,500 warheads. Some arms control analysts and government officials in Washington and Moscow have proposed even further reductions; for example, a START III limit of 1,500 accountable warheads for each state. Russian ratification of START II, finally accomplished in the spring of 2000, was expected to open the door to speedy agreement between the two governments on the even lower START III levels.

Russian ratification of START II and movement toward START III was set back temporarily by NATO's war against Yugoslavia for seventy-eight days in spring 1999. The Russian Duma postponed consideration of ratification of the agreement until October 1999, where it stalled further in the face of Duma elections scheduled for December 1999. Although U.S. officials were frustrated that START approval was melting down in Russian domestic politics, the meltdown was seen by most American experts as a temporary one. Russia cannot afford to modernize a force larger than one that meets START II levels. And there are strong indications in the diplomatic pourparlers between Russians and Americans that Russia would, for economic reasons, prefer lower than START II levels of warheads and delivery systems. In addition to the fact that Russia cannot afford indiscriminate modernization and force building in the next century, Russia also needs Western economic aid, which is more likely to be obtained by the successful completion of mutual arms reductions.

Economics is only one determinant of possible arms control outcomes, however, and not necessarily the most important. Russia's threat perception is equally important if not more so. The end of the Cold War means that political relations between the United States and Russia are not ideologically hostile as they were between the United States and the former Soviet Union. But many Russian military and political leaders remain wedded to Cold War thinking about missile defenses. And the United States announced plans to make a decision about possible NMD (national missile defense of the U.S. territory against accidental launches or light attacks) by 2000, with a possible beginning of NMD deployment in 2005, has increased opposition in Russia to ratification of START II. By itself, Russian concern about U.S. BMD and possible American abrogation of the ABM Treaty of 1972 might not be an arms control "war stopper." But Russian threat perceptions during the Clinton administration were also raised by the enlargement of NATO to include Poland, the Czech Republic, and Hungary in 1999. Russians noted that the formal accession of these states to NATO took place during NATO's air war against Yugoslavia (Operation Allied Force).

Russia's options for modernizing its forces after 1999 will be constrained by the state of its economy. Russian intercontinental ballistic missiles remain the backbone of its strategic retaliatory forces. At the end of 1998 nineteen ICBM bases held 756 missiles of five types: SS-18s, SS-19s, SS-24s, and SS-27s in underground silos; rail-mobile SS-24s; and road-mobile SS-25s. START II entry into force would eliminate all SS-18s and SS-24s and all except 105 SS-19s: remaining SS-19s would be downloaded to a single warhead. Some ICBM silos may be converted to accept the SS-27 Topol-M.[7] General Vladimir Yakovlev, CINC (Commander in Chief) of the Strategic Rocket Forces, called in 1999 for a production schedule of twenty to thirty Topol M (SS-27) becoming operational for each of the next three years, and for thirty to forty per year for the following three years.

With regard to ballistic missile submarines, Russia's START exchange data of 1998 included forty-two submarines of six classes, but the actual number of submarines available and fully operational is fewer than that. The Russian navy considers only twenty-five SSBNs as operational, sixteen in the Northern Fleet and nine in the Pacific Fleet.[8] Operational tempos of the Russian SSBN fleet have been drastically reduced since the end of the Cold War, and Russia might have as few as ten to fifteen operational SSBNs by the end of 2003 (consisting of Delta IVs, newer Delta IIIs, and Typhoons). Although the keel for the first Borey-class SSBN was laid in November 1996, construction was suspended in 1998 at least temporarily amid official statements that the ship was being redesigned.[9] Russia in the autumn of 1998 was already below the START II established ceiling for warheads carried on SLBMs (1,750).

The modernization plans for the Russian strategic-bomber force are as vague as those for the navy. Russia claimed some seventy strategic bombers at the end of 1998, but fewer were actually operational due to lack of funds. The current generation of ALCMs is approaching the end of their service lives, adding an additional modernization requirement for airborne resources already stretched. The commander in chief of the Russian Air Force has announced plans to replace the Tu-95MS Bear H with a new aircraft after 2010, a rather distant date. Only two of the six Tu-160 Blackjack bombers listed as operational at the end of 1998 were actually able to take off, and plans to purchase additional Blackjacks from Ukraine fell through in 1997. The number of operational strategic bombers deployed in the next decade will surely fall below current deployments, and the possibility of Russia's going out of the bomber business entirely cannot be discounted.[10]

U.S. OPTIONS: DATA ANALYSIS

Assured Retaliation

Given reasonable assumptions about projected U.S. defense spending in the first decade of the twenty-first century, the United States will have more options than Russia with regard to the modernization of its strategic nuclear forces. Throughout the Cold War and since it ended, various proposals have been made for reducing force sizes by downsizing the existing triad of strategic nuclear-delivery systems or by reducing the triad to a dyad or monad. Four options are considered here. They offer a range of candidate forces and a mix of alternative basing modes and delivery systems. Some are more politically plausible than others, but we are more interested in their attributes related to the arms race and crisis stability. The options are a balanced triad, a dyad with no ICBMs, a triad with no B-52s, and a force based on sea-based missiles only (force structures are summarized in Appendix A to this chapter).

A mathematical model of force attrition was used to compare the four candidate forces at two possible START III-compliant levels: 2,500 warheads and 1,500 warheads. In the case of each of these eight forces we first compared their maximum and minimum or assured retaliation. Maximum retaliation occurred when forces were on generated alert and launched on warning. Minimum or assured retaliation was characterized by forces on day-to-day alert and launch after riding out the attack.

With 1,500 deployed warheads, the United States can still provide for about 1,200 surviving and arriving warheads against an attack force of comparable size when U.S. forces are in their maximum-retaliation condition of generated alert and launch on warning. There is not a great deal of variation across force structures under conditions of maximum retaliation. On the other hand, if we compare the capability of the various forces to provide for minimum or assured retaliation (day alert and retaliate after riding out the attack), a great deal of variation is apparent. The range of arriving warheads, under the assumption of assured (minimum) retaliation, is from about 400 for the balanced triad to about 800 for the SLBM-only force. An interesting outcome is that the four 1,500-limit forces perform about the same under the condition of generated alert and retaliation after ride out: from 950 to about 1,200 surviving and arriving warheads.

The differences and similarities across force structures at both 2,500 and 1,500 START III-ceilings are summarized graphically in Figures 6.1 and 6.2. Figure 6.1 shows the performance of the four forces under conditions of maximum retaliation. Figure 6.2 shows performance under the assumption of minimum or assured retaliation.

What conclusions are suggested by this analysis? Under conditions of generated alert and launch on warning the composition of forces matters little. Under the opposite, worst-case conditions for the United States as a defender—day-to-day alert and retaliation after ride out—some options clearly outperform others. Assured (minimum) retaliation is best achieved by the SLBM-only force, the balanced triad does the worst, and the no B-52 and no ICBM options are intermediate. Does this mean the United States should shift to a monad based on sea-launched ballistic missiles?

Dynamic Stability and Alternate Force Structures

Although the diversity argument for the triad can be oversold and a case for a dyad (minus ICBMs or one component of the bomber force) can be argued assertively, an SLBM-only force meets strategic and

Figure 6.1
Maximum Retaliation (Generated Alert, Launch on Warning)

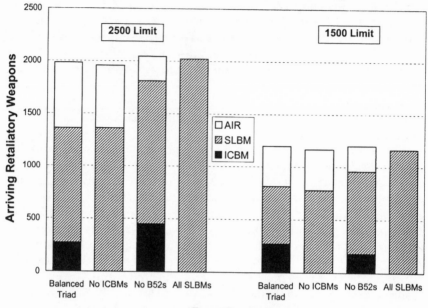

political obstacles. It puts all of the nuclear-retaliatory eggs in one basket of launch vehicles. Although a breakthrough in antisubmarine warfare that would make American SSBNs first-strike vulnerable is unlikely in the next decade or two, it does simplify the attacker's game plan if no land-based missiles or bombers exist to soak up warheads. In addition, from a political standpoint an attacker must strike at the U.S. homeland in order to cause first-strike attrition to the U.S. land-based missile or bomber force. Attacking the American SSBN force does not necessarily involve prompt attacks on the U.S. homeland if enemy ASW can localize and destroy submarines on station or on patrol. Of course, attacking those in port would require detonations on U.S. soil. Another political obstacle to a sea-based monad would be the exclusion of the air force from the mission of strategic nuclear retaliation, a fate certain to be resisted by blue suits with considerable assertiveness.

Perhaps of more practical political and military relevancy are the findings about the performance of the balanced triad compared to a bomber-light triad or to a dyad without ICBMs. Under the assumptions of either maximum or minimum retaliation, the bomber-light triad or dyad of bombers and SSBNs performs as well or better than the triad for larger (2,500) and smaller (1,500) START III-compliant

Figure 6.2
Assured Retaliation (Day-to-Day Alert, Ride Out Attack)

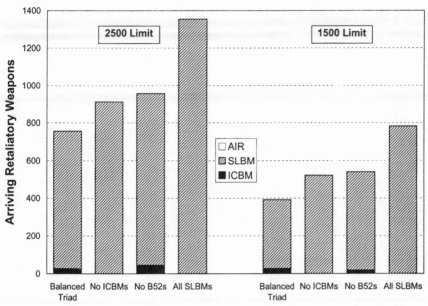

forces. Under worst-case conditions of day alert combined with delayed launch, both the bomber-light triad and the bomber–SSBN dyad
outperform significantly the balanced triad. Is the balanced triad on
its way onto the ash heap of strategic history?

As the song says, "it ain't necessarily so." One must not only compare the ability of each force to provide a certain number of surviving
and arriving warheads. One must consider force qualities in addition
to force outcomes. Among these qualitative attributes, two stand out:
how sensitive or dependent forces are on the requirement for generation, and how sensitive or dependent they are on the need for launch
on warning as opposed to retaliation after ride out. Forces that must
be alerted to be saved from prompt attack may contribute to rising
tensions in the middle of a crisis. Forces that require prompt launch
may stimulate a reciprocal fear of surprise attack leading to a mistaken decision for preemption.

Tables 6.1, 6.2, 6.3, and 6.4 summarize pertinent information about
the deployed, on-line, alerted, surviving, and arriving warheads for
each of four U.S. forces within a 2,500-warhead ceiling for START III.

The most likely mode of retaliation for U.S. forces in a crisis would
be to launch forces already alerted but riding out the attack. Each of
the four force structures can guarantee a retaliatory response in that

Table 6.1
START 3-2500-1; 2,500 Limit; Balanced Triad

GEN/LOW	Deployed	On-Line	Alert	Surviving	Arriving
ICBM	300	300	300	300	270
SLBM	1344	1210	1210	1210	1089
Air	856	770	770	770	624
Total	2500	2280	2280	2280	1983
GEN/ROA					
ICBM	300	300	300	30	27
SLBM	1344	1210	1210	1210	1089
Air	856	770	770	770	624
Total	2500	2280	2280	2010	1740
DAY/LOW					
ICBM	300	300	300	300	270
SLBM	1344	1210	810	810	729
Air	856	770	0	0	0
Total	2500	2280	1110	1110	999
DAY/ROA					
ICBM	300	300	300	30	27
SLBM	1344	1210	810	810	729
Air	856	770	0	0	0
Total	2500	2280	1110	840	756

Source: James Scouras and author.

scenario from 1,600 to 2,000 warheads. Even under the condition of least readiness and maximum surprise, all forces riding out the attack on day alert can still retaliate with some 700 to 1,000 warheads (in round numbers). In this model the balanced triad performs least effectively on day alert and riding out the attack, while the SLBM-only force maximizes the number of arriving warheads. In this regard, the model may not capture some of the synergy for the defender that may result from the complications faced by the attacker in planning simultaneous or sequential attacks against three differently based components of the U.S. strategic nuclear force (see the next section for additional discussion on this point).

Suppose we want to ask a more specific question with regard to the dynamic stability of a nuclear balance: How sensitive is any of the U.S. force structures to the difference between launch on warning and launch after riding out the attack? Some have advocated moving away

Table 6.2
START 3-2500-2; 2,500 Limit; No ICBMs

GEN/LOW	Deployed	On-Line	Alert	Surviving	Arriving
ICBM	0	0	0	0	0
SLBM	1680	1512	1512	1512	1361
Air	816	734	734	734	595
Total	2496	2246	2246	2246	1956
GEN/ROA					
ICBM	0	0	0	0	0
SLBM	1680	1512	1512	1512	1361
Air	816	734	734	734	595
Total	2496	2246	2246	2246	1956
DAY/LOW					
ICBM	0	0	0	0	0
SLBM	1680	1512	1013	1013	912
Air	816	734	0	0	0
Total	2496	2246	1013	1013	912
DAY/ROA					
ICBM	0	0	0	0	0
SLBM	1680	1512	1013	1013	912
Air	816	734	0	0	0
Total	2496	2246	1013	1013	912

Source: James Scouras and author.

from multiple- or even single-warhead ICBMs on account of their first-strike potential combined with their vulnerability if silo based. If START agreements succeed in removing multiple-warhead, land-based missiles from both American and Russian arsenals, the arithmetic of single-warhead ICBMs will favor defenders against attackers (because it will cost the attacker at least one launcher for each warhead destroyed). However, even single-warhead ICBMs based in silos can be destroyed in the early phases of an attack unless they are launched on warning or "under attack" (after some of the attacker's warheads have actually impacted on their targets but before most of the attack arrives). The necessity to rely on prompt launch to save the ICBM force reduces the incentives of policy makers to wait until the last possible moment before ordering a retaliatory strike. In Figure 6.3, the sensitivities of the various forces to launch on warning are compared for 2,500-warhead and 1,500-warhead ceilings.

Table 6.3
START 3-2500-3; 2,500 Limit; No B-52s

GEN/LOW	Deployed	On-Line	Alert	Surviving	Arriving
ICBM	500	500	500	500	450
SLBM	1680	1512	1512	1512	1361
Air	320	288	288	288	233
Total	2500	2300	2300	2300	2044
GEN/ROA					
ICBM	500	500	500	50	45
SLBM	1680	1512	1512	1512	1361
Air	320	288	288	288	233
Total	2500	2300	2300	1850	1639
DAY/LOW					
ICBM	500	500	500	500	450
SLBM	1680	1512	1013	1013	912
Air	320	288	0	0	0
Total	2500	2300	1513	1513	1362
DAY/ROA					
ICBM	500	500	500	50	45
SLBM	1680	1512	1013	1013	912
Air	320	288	0	0	0
Total	2500	2300	1513	1063	957

Source: James Scouras and author.

The balanced and no-B52 triads show significant sensitivity to the difference between prompt and delayed launch. The bomber–SLBM dyad and the all-SLBM force are insensitive to the difference between launch on warning and riding out the attack. This obviously reflects the invulnerability of submarines and the lesser role of ICBMs in these two cases compared to the bomber-light and balanced triads.

BEYOND NUMBER CRUNCHING:
ISSUES OF STRATEGY AND POLICY

What significance do these findings have for a post–Cold War deterrent system characterized by nonhostile political relations between the United States and Russia? One might reasonably argue that nuclear deterrence between the two states is neither necessary nor desirable in the next century. This is certainly the case if favorable-to-U.S. trends

Table 6.4
START 3-2500-4; 2,500 Limit; All SLBMs

GEN/LOW	Deployed	On-Line	Alert	Surviving	Arriving
ICBM	0	0	0	0	0
SLBM	2496	2246	2246	2246	2022
Air	0	0	0	0	0
Total	2496	2246	2246	2246	2022
GEN/ROA					
ICBM	0	0	0	0	0
SLBM	2496	2246	2246	2246	2022
Air	0	0	0	0	0
Total	2496	2246	2246	2246	2022
DAY/LOW					
ICBM	0	0	0	0	0
SLBM	2496	2246	1505	1505	1355
Air	0	0	0	0	0
Total	2496	2246	1505	1505	1355
DAY/ROA					
ICBM	0	0	0	0	0
SLBM	2496	2246	1505	1505	1355
Air	0	0	0	0	0
Total	2496	2246	1505	1505	1355

Source: James Scouras and author.

continue in Russia and Russia moves further toward democracy and a free-market economy. Even if Russia's pathway to democracy and capitalism is full of potholes, any nonimperial Russian regime content to live within its current Federation borders and to practice nonoffensive defense poses no military threat to the United States or to NATO. Deterrence, nuclear style, may have become passé between the two nuclear superpowers of the Cold War.

Perhaps so, given these optimistic expectations. But more pessimistic futures can be imagined between the U.S. and Russian governments. And even optimistic projections must acknowledge that the two states have a shared interest in maintaining essentially equivalent strategic nuclear arsenals and weapons that are superior in quality and in quantity to those of any third party. The new world order will not allow to the Americans or the Russians the nuclear suasion that their forces held over diplomacy in the Cold War. The spread of nuclear and other weapons of mass de-

Figure 6.3
Sensitivity to Launch on Warning

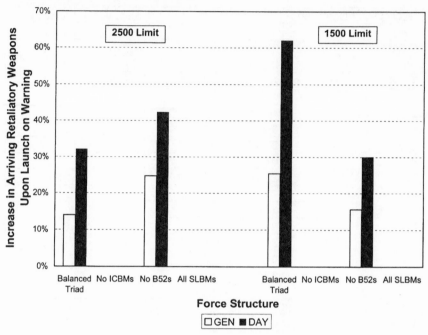

struction together with advanced long-range delivery systems is one of the major threats to world peace in the next century. U.S. and Russian nuclear forces can help to retard the spread of nuclear weapons and long-range ballistic missiles by supporting diplomacy intended to dissuade or discourage rogue states or nonstate actors from acquiring these weapons. Superior (to everyone else) U.S. and Russian nuclear arsenals also provide a disincentive to would-be regional hegemons or aspiring peer competitors. If, for example, American and Russian nuclear forces were reduced in size and diminished in capability to an extent that permitted, say, China to leap forward into nuclear parity within two decades or so, stability in Asia would be diminished and the positions of Taiwan, Indonesia, and Japan less secure.

The idea that peace is supported by continuing American and Russian nuclear strength is one that professional arms controllers and disarmament advocates find hard to take. Equally repugnant to many in the same communities is the possibility that the United States would commit itself to deploy ballistic missile defenses regardless of Russian sentiments or of the need to amend or abrogate the ABM Treaty. The author will not revisit the entire Cold War debate about ballistic missile defenses here. The Cold War debates about BMD were swamped by two exogenous factors: excessive technicism and ideological fanaticism by proponents and opponents. Plainly stated, there was a great deal of lying and sloppy analysis on both sides of the issue.

Answering the question of national missile defense is now important, and it plays into the problem of deciding whether the United States needs a two-sided or three-cornered strategic retaliatory force in the early years of the twenty-first century. If the United States deploys a light system to defend against rogue attacks or accidental launches, it will do so with or without the concurrence of the Russians. Russia is not in a position to prevent the United States from deploying defenses. But Russia can make U.S. and NATO political life more complicated, as in its support or lack thereof for START III, the Comprehensive Test Ban Treaty, and other measures contributory to the reduction of vertical or horizontal nuclear proliferation. The United States also needs Russian cooperation in other matters. The long-term stabilization of Europe and central Eurasia cannot be accomplished without the cooperation of Russia. And the cooperation of Russia will only be obtained if Russia feels secure.

The United States and NATO cannot jeopardize their own security in order to pay homage to Russian insecurity. But they can and must contribute to a realistic conception of Russian security. Russian concerns about the enlargement of NATO to its very borders (Kaliningrad) and those of Ukraine (historically commingled with Russia) are not mere propaganda. NATO includes a nuclear guarantee. And Russian military planners recognize that their underpaid, poorly equipped, and ill-trained conventional forces are ill-suited to the defense of eleven time zones worth of borders. Contiguous to Russia are former Soviet states caught up in political turbulence that has or may soon spill over into Russia itself. Also bordering Russia is China, a major nuclear power with regionally hegemonial ambitions (at least) in the Pacific basin. Parts of Russia caught up in Islamic revolution against Russian rule (Chechnya, Dagestan) are in the volatile Caucasus region located between Russia and Iran. Iran openly seeks to acquire nuclear weapons and ballistic missiles. An Iranian regime armed with nuclear weapons and ballistic missiles of appropriate range would be in a position to counterdeter Russia's incursion against Chechnya as in 1994–1996 and again in the autumn of 1999. An Iranian bomb shared with Afghanistan and Pakistan could create an arc of Islamic extended nuclear deterrence used against Russia or against former Soviet states bordering Iran, Afghanistan, and Pakistan (including oil-rich Turkmenistan on the Caspian Sea). Iranian efforts to develop a nuclear-weapons capability have been supported by China.

Russia can be its own worst enemy, however. Intentions do matter, and the United States is not Iran or China. NATO is not planning any incursion into Russia. And the debate over ballistic missile defenses has gone beyond the "Star Wars" era, with its hubris of near-perfect shields and space armadas. Current U.S. proposals for NMD deployments, possibly to begin in the year 2005, envision ground-based interceptors and other systems that could be deployed in a manner compliant with the ABM Treaty (although not necessarily). The U.S. Congressional and other domestic policy debate on BMD has already shifted its center of gravity away from Cold War–era exclusive emphasis on offensive retaliation for deterrence. Congress has passed several pieces of legislation in the last few years calling upon the Clinton administration to deploy missile defenses as soon as it is feasible to do so, although Congress has not mandated any particular kind of system. Russia's response thus far has been to make veiled or undisguised threats of a renewed offensive arms race: This is old thinking. The United States does not threaten Russia by intention, and will not inadvertently do so if Russia is kept informed of U.S. technology developments and offered an opportunity to share in development and deployment.

Should Russia worry that a U.S. NMD system originally intended for use against rogues could grow into a light BMD system that might be inadequate against Russia's first strike but sufficient to negate a Russian second strike following a U.S. first strike? This would be the functional equivalent of "deterring Russia's deterrent." Some Russians may worry about this possibility, but the United States has little interest in deterring Russia's deterrent unless the character of U.S.–Russian political relations changes drastically from its contemporary (1999) condition. Apart from politics, would the very existence of a U.S. NMD technology create the sum of its own fears? The United States might have reason to be fearful of Russian fears, but for reasons having less to do with quantities of warheads than with qualitative issues related to crisis stability. If the Russian START III force is less crisis stable than its U.S. counterpart, the Russian military and political leadership may be more inclined to engage in provocative alerting behaviors or to initiate nuclear use as a last resort.

In Figure 6.4, U.S. and Soviet/Russian Cold War (1991), START I, START II, and START III forces are compared according to their degree of dependency (sensitivity) to force generation. Sensitivity is measured by the percentage difference between ungenerated and generated surviving and arriving warheads in each case.

Each of Russia's forces is more sensitive to the differences between generated and ungenerated alert conditions than its American counterpart. And Russia's forces are more sensitive to their degree of alertness when they are riding out an attack compared to when they are launched on warning.

Russia's greater dependency on force generation becomes even more significant if that condition is complemented by a greater reliance, compared to the United States, on launch on warning for force survivability. Figure 6.5 examines how sensitive Russia's Cold War, START I, START II,

Figure 6.4
Sensitivity to Generation

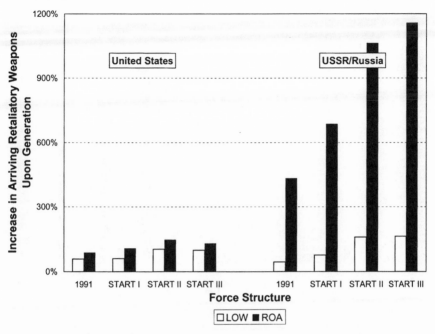

and START III forces are to the difference between launch on warning and retaliation after riding out the attack, compared to U.S. forces.

Russian forces on generated alert are not much more sensitive to launch on warning than U.S. counterparts. But each Russian force on day alert is much more sensitive than the American force of similar size. Russian START III forces on day alert and not launching under attack (riding out the attack) could provide 200 or fewer warheads surviving and arriving at their intended U.S. targets. This number would still be absolutely devastating from a U.S. standpoint. But Russians, contemplating the scenario of a U.S. first strike accompanied by a limited NMD system, could fear the neutralization of their deterrent if the U.S. system were expanded while Russia failed to modernize its offensive retaliatory forces.

CONCLUSIONS

From the standpoint of arms control per se, it might be more cost effective to reduce the venerable U.S. triad to a dyad or even a single missile force based on submarines. Strategy is more complicated. It assumes a reactive opponent who is working to defeat your strategy. U.S. military planners are therefore almost certain to resist a monad as

Figure 6.5
Sensitivity to Launch on Warning

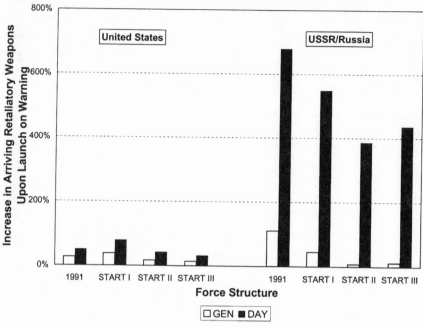

inviting an all-out research-and-development effort to make it obsolete. On the other hand, the strategy-driven case against a dyad compared to a triad is not so clear. A dyad of U.S. bomber-delivered weapons and submarine-launched missiles fulfills the requirements of assured destruction and target coverage at START III levels·as well as a triad does. It can be argued that U.S. single-warhead land-based missiles act as a warhead sponge: The enemy must make a large attack against the continental United States or none at all. This is true mathematically, but ignores the symbolism that even a single detonation in anger on American national territory would have. An attacker would have to assume that a devastating and unacceptable retaliation would be just as likely from attacks on submarine and bomber bases as from additional and even more destructive attacks on ICBM fields. One Pearl Harbor would suffice.

NOTES

I am grateful to Dr. James Scouras, Strategy Research Group, for providing a model developed by him to generate tables and charts used in this chapter. He bears no responsibility for its application here, nor for any results or arguments. Projections assume, for analysis, that both states deployed, or might deploy, weapons close to the START I, START II, and START III limits, even if the assumption is politically inexact.

1. General Aleksandr Lebed, former national security advisor to Russian President Boris Yeltsin, claimed in a U.S. network television interview in September 1997 that many portable "suitcase" nuclear weapons (atomic demolition munitions; ADMs) created during the Cold War for use with Soviet special-operations forces could not be accounted for by the Russian military now. The U.S. *60 Minutes* program of September 6 raised the possibility that missing weapons could have been sold to terrorists or states like Iraq with nuclear ambitions. Russian defense officials denied that any nuclear weapons were unaccounted for.

2. John Erickson, "'Russia Will Not be Trifled With': Geopolitical Facts and Fantasies," *Journal of Strategic Studies* 22 (1999): 242–268, esp. 253.

3. RFE/RL Newsline, vol. 3, no. 197, part I, 8 October 1999, <newsline@list. rferl.org>.

4. Martin Nesirsky, "Short of Conventional Weapons, Russia Reassesses Security Strategy," *Russia Today*, <http://www.russiatoday.com>, 10 October 1999.

5. *Reuters* Moscow, 12 October 1999, via *Russia Today*, <http://www.russia today.com>, 12 October 1999.

6. See Center for Counterproliferation Research, National Defense University, and Center for Global Security Research, Lawrence Livermore National Laboratory, *U.S. Nuclear Policy in the 21st Century: A Fresh Look at National Strategy and Requirements* (Washington, D.C.: U.S. Government Printing Office, 1998), 3.12–3.15, for a summary of arguments for the U.S. strategic nuclear triad.

7. *National Resources Defense Council Nuclear Notebook* 55, no. 2 (1999).

8. Ibid.

9. Ibid.

10. Ibid.

APPENDIX A:
U.S. TRIAD AND ALTERNATIVE FORCES

START III   Balanced Triad   2500 Limit

Platform Name	Deployed Platforms	SNDVs per Platform	Warheads per SNDV	Deployed Warheads
MM III	300	1	1	300
Total ICBM	**300**			**300**
Trident D-5	14	24	4	1344
Total SLBM	**14**			**1344**
B52H	65	1	8	520
B2	21	1	16	336
Total Air	**86**			**856**
Grand Total				**2500**

Appendix A (*continued*)

START III No ICBMs 2500 Limit				
Platform Name	Deployed Platforms	SNDVs per Platform	Warheads per SNDV	Deployed Warheads
None				
Total ICBM	**0**			**0**
Trident D-5	14	24	5	1680
Total SLBM	**14**			**1680**
B52H	60	1	8	480
B2	21	1	16	336
Total Air	**81**			**816**
Grand Total				**2496**

Appendix A (*continued*)

START III No B-52s 2500 Limit				
Platform Name	**Deployed Platforms**	**SNDVs per Platform**	**Warheads per SNDV**	**Deployed Warheads**
MM III	500	1	1	500
Total ICBM	**500**			**500**
Trident D-5	14	24	5	1680
Total SLBM	**14**			**1680**
B2	20	1	16	320
Total Air	**20**			**320**
Grand Total				**2500**

Appendix A (*continued*)

START III All SLBMs 2500 Limit				
Platform Name	**Deployed Platforms**	**SNDVs per Platform**	**Warheads per SNDV**	**Deployed Warheads**
None				
Total ICBM	**0**			**0**
Trident D-5	13	24	8	2496
Total SLBM	**13**			**2496**
None				
Total Air	**0**			**0**
Grand Total				**2496**

START III All SLBMs 1500 Limit				
Platform Name	**Deployed Platforms**	**SNDVs per Platform**	**Warheads per SNDV**	**Deployed Warheads**
None				
Total ICBM	**0**			**0**
Trident D-5	12	24	5	1440
Total SLBM	**12**			**1440**
None				
Total Air	**0**			**0**
Grand Total				**1440**

Appendix A (*continued*)

START III Balanced Triad 1500 Limit				
Platform Name	**Deployed Platforms**	**SNDVs per Platform**	**Warheads per SNDV**	**Deployed Warheads**
MM III	300	1	1	300
Total ICBM	**300**			**300**
Trident D-5	7	24	4	672
Total SLBM	**7**			**672**
B52H	24	1	8	192
B2	21	1	16	336
Total Air	**45**			**528**
Grand Total				**1500**

Appendix A (*continued*)

START III No ICBMs 1500 Limit				
Platform Name	Deployed Platforms	SNDVs per Platform	Warheads per SNDV	Deployed Warheads
None				
Total ICBM	**0**			**0**
Trident D-5	10	24	4	960
Total SLBM	**10**			**960**
B52H	25	1	8	200
B2	21	1	16	336
Total Air	**46**			**536**
Grand Total				**1496**

Appendix A (*continued*)

START III No B52s 1500 Limit				
Platform Name	Deployed Platforms	SNDVs per Platform	Warheads per SNDV	Deployed Warheads
MM III	200	1	1	200
Total ICBM	**200**			**200**
Trident D-5	10	24	4	960
Total SLBM	**10**			**960**
B2	21	1	16	336
Total Air	**21**			**336**
Grand Total				**1496**

Source: James Scouras and author.

APPENDIX B:
U.S. AND RUSSIAN/SOVIET
COLD WAR AND START FORCES

US 1991

Platform Name	Deployed Platforms	SNDVs per Platform	Warheads per SNDV	Deployed Warheads
MMII	450	1	1	450
MM III	200	1	3	600
MM IIIa	300	1	3	900
Peacekeeper	50	1	10	500
Total ICBM	**1000**			**2450**
Poseidon C3	10	16	10	1600
Poseidon C4	12	16	8	1536
Trident C4	8	24	8	1536
Trident D5	3	24	8	576
Total SLBM	**33**			**5248**
B52G	46	1	12	552
B52H	95	1	20	1900
B1B	97	1	16	1552
Total Air	**238**			**4004**
Grand Total				**11702**

Appendix B (*continued*)

US START I				
Platform Name	**Deployed Platforms**	**SNDVs per Platform**	**Warheads per SNDV**	**Deployed Warheads**
MM III	200	1	3	600
MM IIIa	300	1	3	900
Peacekeeper	50	1	10	500
Total ICBM	**550**			**2000**
Trident C4	8	24	8	1536
Trident D5	10	24	8	1920
Total SLBM	**18**			**3456**
B52H	71	1	20	1420
B2	21	1	16	336
Total Air	**92**			**1756**
Grand Total				**7212**

Appendix B (*continued*)

US START II				
Platform Name	**Deployed Platforms**	**SNDVs per Platform**	**Warheads per SNDV**	**Deployed Warheads**
MM III	500	1	1	500
Total ICBM	**500**			**500**
Trident D5	14	24	5	1680
Total SLBM	**14**			**1680**
B52H (20 alcm)	34	1	20	680
B52H (8 alcm)	37	1	8	296
B2	21	1	16	336
Total Air	**92**			**1312**
Grand Total				**3492**

Appendix B (*continued*)

US START III				
Platform Name	Deployed Platforms	SNDVs per Platform	Warheads per SNDV	Deployed Warheads
MM II	300	1	1	300
Total ICBM	**300**			**300**
Poseidon C3	14	24	4	1344
Total SLBM	**14**			**1344**
B52G	65	1	8	520
B52H	21	1	16	336
Total Air	**86**			**856**
Grand Total				**2500**

Appendix B (*continued*)

USSR 1991

Platform Name	Deployed Platforms	SNDVs per Platform	Warheads per SNDV	Deployed Warheads
SS-11	326	1	1	326
SS-13	40	1	1	40
SS-17	47	1	4	188
SS-18	308	1	10	3080
SS-19	300	1	6	1800
SS-24 (silo)	56	1	10	560
SS-24 (rail)	33	1	10	330
SS-25	288	1	1	288
Total ICBM	**1398**			**6612**
Yankee I	12	16	1	192
Delta I	18	12	1	216
Delta II	4	16	1	64
Yankee II	1	12	1	12
Delta III	14	16	3	672
Typhoon	6	20	10	1200
Delta IV	7	16	4	448
Total SLBM	**62**			**2804**
Bear A,B,G	63	1	2	126
Bear H (6 alcm)	27	1	6	162
Bear H (16 alcm)	57	1	16	912
Blackjack	15	1	12	180
Total Air	**162**			**1380**
Grand Total				**10796**

Appendix B (*continued*)

| | | SNDVs | Warheads | |
| RF START I | | | | |
Platform Name	Deployed Platforms	per Platform	per SNDV	Deployed Warheads
SS-18	154	1	10	1540
SS-24 (rail)	36	1	10	360
SS-25 (silo)	270	1	1	270
SS-25 (road)	400	1	1	400
Total ICBM	**860**			**2570**
Typhoon	6	20	10	1200
Delta IV	7	16	4	448
Borey	6	16	6	576
Total SLBM	**19**			**2224**
Bear H (6 alcm)	29	1	6	174
Bear H (16 alcm)	35	1	16	560
Blackjack	6	1	12	72
Total Air	**70**			**806**
Grand Total	**949**			**5600**

RF START II

Platform Name	Deployed Platforms	SNDVs per Platform	Warheads per SNDV	Deployed Warheads
SS-25 (silo)	270	1	1	270
SS-25 (road)	630	1	1	630
Total ICBM	**900**			**900**
Delta IV	7	16	4	448
Borey	14	16	6	1344
Total SLBM	**21**			**1792**
Bear H (6 alcm)	29	1	6	174
Bear H (16 alcm)	35	1	16	560
Blackjack	6	1	12	72
Total Air	**70**			**806**
Grand Total	**991**			**3498**

Appendix B (*continued*)

Platform Name	Deployed Platforms	SNDVs per Platform	Warheads per SNDV	Deployed Warheads
RF START III				
SS-25/27 (silo)	270	1	1	270
SS-25/27 (road)	400	1	1	400
Total ICBM	**670**			**670**
Delta IV	7	16	4	448
Borey	6	16	6	576
Total SLBM	**13**			**1024**
Bear H (6 alcm)	29	1	6	174
Bear H (16 alcm)	35	1	16	560
Blackjack	6	1	12	72
Total Air	**70**			**806**
Grand Total	**753**			**2500**

Source: James Scouras and author.

7

Conclusion

Stephen J. Cimbala

Contributors to this volume were asked the evaluate the future of deterrence, of proliferation, or both. This chapter summarizes what we have learned and what implications these findings may hold for theory and policy. Although insights from all contributors have influenced what is written here, the editor bears sole responsibility for these arguments and opinions.

Nuclear deterrence is not dead, like the Soviet Union, or obsolete, like hula hoops. Nuclear deterrence remains important for global security because nuclear weapons are still there and, even if they were not, the knowledge of how to build nuclear weapons would be. What has ended is the U.S.–Soviet global geopolitical and ideological competition. Nuclear deterrence in the twenty-first century, therefore, will not be focused on avoiding a major conventional war in Europe or on preventing massive exchanges of weapons between North Dakota and Siberia.

NUCLEAR WEAPONS AND DETERRENCE IN THE COLD WAR

The Cold War emphasis on deterring a major war in Europe and/or a conflict between the Americans and Soviets created a certain bias, not to say laziness, in analysis. As the numbers of survivable weapons in American and Soviet arsenals grew into many thousands, it became clear that there would be no winners or even Phyrric victors in a nuclear war. The task was war avoidance by means of nuclear threat. This nuclear bargaining could become quite sinister and dangerous at times, as in major superpower crises. But most of the time nuclear weapons just stood there in their silos or in bomb racks, silent sentinels reminding their purveyors of the imminent Armageddon that would almost certainly follow the first detonations in anger.

The U.S.–Soviet duopoly over large and survivable nuclear forces was one very important and unique aspect of nuclear deterrence as it was practiced during Cold War. Another unique aspect was the absence of any countervailing defenses for nuclear offenses. For most of history the introduction of new offensive weapons had been followed by eventual breakthroughs in defensive countermeasures that might nullify those more-threatening offenses. But the predominance of nuclear rocket missiles in the Cold War seemed to nullify this law of historical yin and yang between offensive and defensive technologies. The gap between offenses and defensive technologies was so wide as to invite ridicule, at least in the United States, of efforts to deploy national missile defenses (Reagan's program was dubbed "Star Wars" by critics and the media) or to develop a national civil-defense plan to cope with the effects of nuclear war. It seemed to Cold War strategists that as far as the technology eye could see ahead, defenses against nuclear attack were either wasteful or counterproductive to stability.[1]

Stability, in fact, became a new term of art in strategy, at least insofar as strategy coupled with nuclear arms control. Stability was thought by most American analysts and policy makers to rest on a U.S.–Soviet mutual hostage relationship based on offensive retaliation. A stable deterrent was one that could guarantee assured destruction of the opponent's society in revenge, regardless of the size or scale of the attack or the reason for the attack: for example, from fear of being attacked as opposed to a cold-blooded decision to launch a preventive war. The Great Deterrent was thus automated politically as well as technically.

Of course, as the numbers of American and Soviet nuclear weapons grew apace during the Cold War, the option presented itself to exceed minimum speed limits based on "assured destruction" of the opponent's society. The Soviet leadership looked at matters military and strategic through a different prism compared to the American leadership. The Soviet Union had had a different historical experience, of invasion and of temporary occupation, and operated from a different set of premises about the sources of global conflict. Conflict, in the Soviet view, was based on ideological incompatibility between capitalist and socialist systems. Weapons were symptoms of conflict, not causes of it. The possibility that the alliance of capitalist states embodied in NATO might initiate a war at any time could not be excluded.

The Soviet Union therefore had to be prepared for another Barbarossa, including a possibly nuclear one.

Thus, although the Soviet leadership of the Cold War years acknowledged the significance of nuclear weapons (after Stalin) and the reality of nuclear deterrence, deterrence was never the experiment in applied psychology or the substitute for war preparedness for Moscow that it appeared to be in Washington. Actually, nuclear deterrence in Washington was influenced from two sides: the technological, driven by the air force, and the social scientific, originating in government-supported think tanks studying military problems out from under the control of the brass hats. The newly independent air force was anxious to demonstrate that, while the army and navy might have some roles in future warfare, air power had become the premier arm of service and it would be air power that would deliver the Sunday punch in the Great Deterrent. So pervasive was the air force hold on military thinking in the early years of the Cold War that the army and navy competed to outdo air power for strategic (i.e., long range and massive destruction) missions. The navy finally attained its own nuclear-retaliation force in Polaris and successor generations of ballistic missile submarines; the army acquired property rights to ballistic missile defense, at least on the ground. Missiles were divided among all three arms of service, depending on mission and range.

The other source of influence on the American concepts of nuclear strategy and deterrence was social-scientific thinking from universities, laboratories, and think tanks. The "good news" about this infusion of ideas and expertise from outside the military was that it provided fresh thinking that guarded against military command-mindedness and stand-patism. On the other hand, the ideas of social scientists like Bernard Brodie, Henry Kissinger, and Herman Kahn drew a line between prenuclear and nuclear-strategic thinking that bred distrust among military professionals. Many serving officers exposed to the new thinking were wary because the new concepts seemed to take insufficient cognizance of military history. Others objected to the apparent disparagement of combat experience on the part of some of the new nuclear strategists. Still other military traditionalists were offended by the analytical methods and cult mentality of some of the more quantitative social-scientific strategists, including those who clustered around Secretary of Defense Robert S. McNamara.

There were, until the advent of Mikhail Gorbachev at the top of the Soviet leadership in 1985, no similar coteries of academic social-science thinkers with pervasive influence on the making of military strategy in Moscow. The formulation of military strategy in Moscow, including possible strategy for the use of nuclear weapons in combat, was the responsibility of a very circumscribed political and military elite. Their experience in World War II drove their thinking about military strategy, and their experience in Soviet bureaucracy was not one that encouraged innovation (unless approved by higher echelons) or the importation of thinking about military science or military art from the civilian world.

The preceding statements should not be interpreted to disparage the Soviet approach to military thinking or their writings about strategy during the Cold War. To the contrary, Soviet thinking about the relationship between war and politics and about the historical relationship between weapons and warfare was at least on a par with, if not superior to, its American and allied Western counterparts. The point here is not the subtlety or sophistication of Soviet compared to American military thinking, but the difference in sociological origins and the resulting disparities in emphasis and in conceptual framework.[2] From the Soviet perspective, history showed that war was a normal feature of international life, and their nuclear-armed adversaries could not be trusted not to wage war against them if the conditions seemed propitious. The American view of nuclear weapons, on the other hand, was more absolutist: They would not be employed unless and until the bad guys attacked the good guys, and then a righteous fist of Armageddon would be used to annihilate the bad guys.

The U.S. problem in this regard was not so much in convincing Moscow that its deterrent threats were meaningful with regard to an attack on American soil, but in extending that nuclear deterrent threat to protect U.S. allies in NATO Europe. The deployment of U.S. nuclear weapons in Western Europe was intended to convince the Soviet leadership that no war started there could remain small or nonnuclear. Therefore, it was too risky for them to undertake. On the other hand, this required that the U.S. president offer an unconditional guarantee in peacetime that, in the event of crisis or war, the president might prefer to emphasize in degrees. Nuclear weapons, as the French emphasized in creating their own independent nuclear force, did not lend themselves to subdivision or partialing out of effects. And if the Soviet Union really believed that a conventional military attack across the Fulda Gap automatically led to a series of nuclear exchanges between Montana and Siberia, then it paid Soviet attackers to begin with the most massive attack possible against the American homeland and against the widest target set of U.S. strategic nuclear forces.

There was no way around the logical trade-off between firebreaks, separating conventional from nuclear war in Europe, and coupling, requiring an indivisible deterrent from the inter-German border to the Great Plains of North America. The United States under the Kennedy and Johnson administrations eventually opted for "flexible response" as a declaratory strategy. Officially adopted by NATO in 1967 at the

Americans' behest, it proposed a graduated chain of escalation from an initial phase of conventional war, to the limited use of nuclear weapons in Europe, to the unlimited use of nuclear weapons in global warfare. This great chain of nuclear being was supposed to deter any Soviet aggression in Europe regardless of its political cause or urgency.

Since no World War III took place between 1946 and 1989, many credit nuclear weapons and nuclear deterrence, as explained, for the absence of major war in Europe and of world war for a half century. Given the turbulence of the first half of the twentieth century, the pacification of Europe and the absence of world war are singular accomplishments. But are they probative evidence that nuclear deterrence worked? One might argue that the Americans, Europeans, and Soviets had been exhausted by the exertions of World War II and had neither the intent nor the societal stamina to fight another major war after 1945. This argument of postwar political and societal combat exhaustion has some plausibility for the early years of the Cold War, say until about 1958 or 1959. By then another generation of leaders in the Kremlin and in Washington had come to power and the economies of the United States, the Soviet Union, and Western Europe had recovered from much of their wartime devastation. Memories of World War II U.S.–Soviet accord were replaced by confrontations between 1958 and 1962 over Berlin and Cuba, the latter arguably the most dangerous confrontation of the Cold War.

It is important for predicting the post–Cold War role of nuclear weapons and nuclear deterrence to neither exaggerate nor disparage the status of nuclear weapons in keeping the Cold War peace.[3] Any correct assessment of that role runs into an irony: History turned favorably on the difference, instead of the similarity, in U.S. and Soviet military thinking. If the Americans and Soviets had thought alike about nuclear strategy during the Cold War, then Armageddon might have been closer and the likelihood of actual shooting between the two superpowers much greater.

Because U.S. notions of nuclear strategy were influenced by technology, military servicism, and social-scientific thinking in a weird package fashion, they kept some restraints on the buildup of superfluous weapons and on defense spending. U.S. perspectives on defense strategy also kept open the door to U.S.–Soviet arms control negotiations that helped to mitigate some of the suspicions of the Cold War. On the other hand, the Soviet military traditionalist view of the role of weapons in strategy and its assumption of ideologically driven global conflict made the Soviet leadership cautious and pessimistic about nuclear brinkmanship, threats that left "something to chance," and other manipulations of risk that the Brezhnev regime attributed to Khrushchev in retrospect as "adventurism." Risk-acceptant behavior with nuclear weapons was not, in the Soviet view, prudent unless the issue was deadly serious. Using nuclear weapons to send signals of resolve or of tacit nuclear bargaining in crises was tantamount to playing with atomic fire that might bring down the Soviet regime.

There is another important issue here, related to the role of nuclear weapons in the Cold War and what it might mean for the post–Cold War world. The Soviet leadership, steeped in the tenets of Lenin and Clausewitz, did not believe in apolitical wars. Wars, even nuclear war, grew from political causes having to do with the conflict between socialism and capitalism. Soviet military "doctrine" was always a much more theoretically embedded notion than its usage in Western terminology, where doctrine was characteristically expressed in training manuals. Soviet military doctrine existed at two levels: the sociopolitical and the military–technical. The sociopolitical level of doctrine defined the nature and causes of future war and identified the main enemies of the Soviet Union and their aims. Doctrine at the military–technical level described the ways and means by which Soviet military power could overcome its enemies.[4]

A correct understanding of the role of military doctrine in Soviet policy leads to two important insights. First, the Soviet leadership disbelieved in automated wars. Second, the possibility of accidental or inadvertent nuclear war, while occasionally alluded to in Soviet writing, was not taken as seriously as it was in the West. The differences between the United States and the Soviet Union on these points were more than a matter of semantics. The differences on automatic or accidental nuclear war reflected the differences in the relationship between the state and the armed forces in the two countries. The Soviet armed forces were a politicized entity. The leading military cadres were carefully vetted for their Communist Party bona fides and scrutinized by the main political administration with regard to their career patterns. Additional security organs outside the military were also used to establish the sincerity or at least acquiescence to Party norms on the part of the military leadership. Over time, the Soviet military establishment became more Marxist–Leninist than many members of the Party leadership or government, because they identified the survival of the ideology with the survival of the state, their primary mission.

On account of this, it was impermissible from the perspective of the Soviet political or military leaderships throughout the Cold War for wars to start accidentally or to run automatically. The notion that political leaders, having decided upon a war, turn decisions about military operations over to the armed forces was simply unacceptable to disciples of Lenin as tutored by Clausewitz. This was as true of a war in which nuclear weapons might be used as of any other conflict. Soviet leaders were not fools. They knew how destructive a nuclear war in Europe or a larger war might be. But they also believed in their interpretation of the relationship between war and history. War might be unleashed against the Soviet Union at any time. Preparedness for war, including the conduct of a war through its various phases, was necessary in order to ensure the historically necessary triumph of socialism over capitalism.

The notion of accidentally caused and automatically run wars was a Western idea, not a Soviet one. Nuclear weapons raised popular fears in the United States and in NATO Europe of a mad general grabbing control of the deterrent and launching a Strangelovian attack against Russia. More realistically, there were from time to time mishaps that took place in the operation of nuclear forces that could have led, under less-propitious circumstances, to greater tensions between Washington and Moscow. But this issue was a point of agreement, not disagreement, between the U.S. and Soviet leaderships. Everyone agreed that a mistaken radar warning or a faulty silicon chip in the NORAD computers should not lead to an outbreak of tensions or fighting.

On the other hand, the two states' political and military leaderships were more different in their handling of the issue of automated war. The United States, in order to get around the problem of interservice disputation in the development of nuclear-war plans, created the Single Integrated Operational Plan (SIOP) in the late 1950s. The SIOP was a highly technical and closely held document put together by the Joint Strategic Target Planning Staff (JSTPS) under loose policy guidance from the Department of Defense and the Joint Chiefs of Staff. As the numbers of U.S. nuclear weapons expanded into the thousands and then the tens of thousands, the number of targets identified as ground zeros in the USSR also increased proportionately. The SIOP eventually became so large and complex that it was a nuclear version of the Schlieffen plan. In order to make it workable, the decisions about weapons and targets were worked out in detail and packaged in one or more attack "options" for presidential decision.

In the event of a crisis involving the possible launch of U.S. nuclear weapons, the president would have minutes in which to decide among several major-attack or limited-attack options. But even the limited options involved large numbers of strikes into Eastern Europe and/or Soviet territory, and there was no opportunity for improvisation of plans or options within the plausible time frame of decision. SIOP targeting decisions were based on the requirement in all instances to attain Damage Expectancies (DEs) against various classes of targets. The mechanics of the process drove the compilation of the war plan. Policy planners in the office of the secretary of defense supposedly provided substantive guidance within which the target planners at Omaha were to work. In practice, this guidance was either vague or ineffective. The air force did its thing: It prepared a war plan for the destruction of the Soviet Union's military forces, military-supporting infrastructure, and economy, regardless of the exigent circumstances. The president's decision would essentially be a "yes" or "no."

The Soviet political leadership distrusted its military and feared the emergence of any Red Napoleons with political ambitions, despite the close monitoring and indoctrination of the military by the Party and its security organs. Therefore, the idea of letting a nuclear war run itself by a single predetermined plan was anathema to the Party leadership. In contrast to the rigidity of U.S. nuclear war plans (until the very end of the Cold War, in the Bush administration), the Soviet planning process emphasized requisite variety in options and military tasking. Because war might come in many sizes and shapes and unexpectedly from the Soviet standpoint, leaders had to have more than one major attack option and many minor ones as well.[5] Of course, the United States had these additional options *technically*, but the differences in style of thinking are the issue here. The Soviet political leadership expected that the general staff would run any war hands on, under the close supervision of the Politburo over the purposes of fighting and over the means of battle. Their model would be the Great Patriotic War and Stalin's oversight of his generals during that conflict. While Stalin was forced to concede some things to the professionalism of his general staff and leading field commanders if he wanted to win the war, he did not concede his right to determine the sequence of main political and military objectives nor the costs that the Soviet Union would be willing to bear to obtain them.

NUCLEAR WEAPONS AND DETERRENCE
AFTER THE COLD WAR

What are the implications of these arguments for the post–Cold War world and for Russia, having inherited the former Soviet nuclear arsenal? Do contemporary Russian political and military leaders approach these problems from the same frame of reference as their Soviet predecessors? From the standpoint of the political side of military doctrine, obviously not. Russia is no longer a Communist state and its military is no longer run by Party-approved marshals. But what about the military–technical aspects of doctrine? Is the current or future Russian view of nuclear war, deterrence, or arms control likely to resemble the Soviet one?

We have less than a decade of information to go on here. But it is already apparent that the view of the Putin government (a stand-in for the "Russian" view) compared to that of the Soviet Union on nuclear matters involves continuity in some respects and discontinuity in others. An example of discontinuity is the attitude of Russia toward nuclear first use. An illustration of continuity is the Russian attitude toward national ballistic missile defense and the ABM Treaty.

Soviet renunciation of nuclear first use was a Cold War staple. The Kremlin's apparently superior conventional forces deployable for any war in Europe were thought to place the onus of nuclear first use on NATO. At least this was the accepted wisdom of U.S. and allied threat assessments, and the Soviets took advantage of this NATO assumption of its own conventional inferiority to score propaganda points by officially renouncing nuclear first use for its public appeal. Whether in the event of war the Soviet leadership would have conceded to NATO the actual opportunity for first use and the possible military advantages that went along with it is not so clear. Regardless of counterfactual speculation about what the Soviets might have done in the past, Russia for the present and future has abandoned any pretense of nuclear forbearance.

To the contrary, Russia's official military doctrine states that it may employ nuclear weapons if Russia is attacked by any nuclear-armed state or by a nonnuclear state allied with a nuclear state. In addition, the line between nuclear first use and first strike was an accepted canon by both sides during the Cold War. First use was understood to apply to tactical or operational–tactical nuclear weapons whose flight paths remained within a single theater of military operations. First strike referred to the strategic deterrent forces of the United States and the Soviet Union aimed primarily at one another's homelands. Although the Soviet leadership always denied that any war in Europe could be kept from spreading into a world war as a matter of their deterrence policy vis-á-vis NATO, in practice their military exercises and training reflected a clear understanding of the difference between first use and first strike and the more dangerous character of the latter. In contemporary Russia the line between first use and first strike is less distinct than it was for Soviet leaders and military planners.

Russia's conventional military inferiority compared to NATO is a reversal of the Cold War military relationship and forces Russia into heavier reliance upon its nuclear weapons to compensate. The vaunted Red Army is now a hollow shell that has been pushed back to a Western defense perimeter approximately along the line St. Petersburg–Smolensk–Rostov. NATO now includes Poland, Hungary, and the Czech Republic among its members, so they are covered by NATO's defense guarantee, including the use of nuclear weapons if necessary. NATO has announced that it has no plan, no reason, and no intention of deploying nuclear weapons in any of the Visegrad states, but Russians know that intentions have a way of changing. As if to advertise Russia's apparent military weakness, NATO's bombing campaign against Yugoslavia in the spring of 1999 went on despite remonstrations from Yeltsin and other top Russian leaders. Russia was finally forced to play the humiliating role of diplomatic go-between, assigning former Prime Minister Viktor Chernomyrdin to mediate between Serbian President Milosevic and NATO. NATO's ability to wage war against Yugoslavia in 1999 over a matter of security policy *internal* to a Balkan state that was a traditional ally of Russia was a 1999 version of the Battle of Narva, in which early eighteenth-century Swedes reminded Peter the Great that Russia was not yet a military power to be reckoned with outside of her own borders.

Wesley Clark was no Charles XII. NATO's successful coercion of Milosevic was not the result of heroic leadership on the ground, but of superior defense technology that is at least a generation ahead of cash-starved and backward Russia. In fact, Operation Allied Force demonstrated an embarrassing gap within NATO itself between the U.S. capability for high-technology, information-based conventional warfare and that of her allies. Russia stole some late diplomatic thunder when her peacekeeping forces sneaked into Pristina ahead of NATO's after military operations against Yugoslavia had been concluded. But this was small consolation after the fact of Serbia's humiliation, and Russia's by implication. In an article published in December 1999 on "The Basis of Russia's Military Doctrine," Major General Anatoly Klimenko, Director of the Russian Defense Ministry's Center for Military–Strategic Studies, pointed to the United States "desire to retain its dominant positions in the world" as a destabilizing factor, and added, with regard to NATO, "NATO's policy of destroying [the] existing international security system, expanding its influence and conducting military actions without the approval of the U.N. Security Council challenges international relations and threatens international stability. Moreover, a revival of military confrontation in Europe, and an emergence of large-scale wars is a possible outcome."[6]

The timing of NATO enlargement to coincide with Operation Allied Force, another advertisement of Russia's military impotence, will have important and unfortunate political side effects. One of these will be the further strengthening of hawks in Russia's Duma and Security Council, who have already written off the post–Cold War model of U.S.–Russian military collaboration. Another consequence will be that Russia will continue to rely on its nuclear forces to cover all bets and will find the cash to modernize those forces even at the cost of starving the remainder of its military. The irony of Russia's "get tough" approach to Chechen invasion of Dagestan in the autumn and winter of 1999 was that, while it was conducted with somewhat more tactical shrewdness and political sagacity than the campaign from 1994 through 1996, it nevertheless showed how inadequate the armed forces of Russia would be for waging of any serious campaign outside of Russia's own borders. This situation brings nuclear weapons further forward among Russia's available military options for theater war on its periphery.

If discontinuity is the pattern between Soviet and Russian approaches to nuclear first use, then continuity is more apparent in Russia's stance on national ballistic missile defenses. Russia's representations to U.S. diplomats in START negotiations have been consistently negative with regard to any amendment to the ABM Treaty of 1972. That treaty, signed by the Soviet Union but accepted as obligatory by the Russian Federation as the nuclear successor of the USSR, limits both the United States and the Soviet Union to a single ground-based missile-defense site. The ABM Treaty also precludes either side from developing or deploying a comprehensive system for the defense of its state territory. The United States has indicated to Russia a desire to explore the possibility of one or more amendments to the treaty in order to permit deployment of limited NMD by either state or by both.

The American interest in a possible deployment of NMD is sparked by recognition that the nature of the nuclear threat against the United States or allied European national territory has changed with the end of the Cold War and the demise of the Soviet Union. The threat is primarily one posed by the possibility of limited strikes, either accidental launches or deliberate attacks from rogue states such as North Korea, Iran, Iraq, or Libya. The spread of ballistic missiles and other modern delivery systems to states that are also attempting to acquire or have acquired significant quantities of weapons of mass destruction (nuclear, biological, or chemical weapons) was emphasized by the Clinton administration's counterproliferation policy and by the authoritative Rumsfeld Commission report in 1999.[7] Additional new aspects to the nuclear threat are presented by the post–Cold War growth in Chinese nuclear forces, along with China's apparent intent to contest U.S. maritime predominance in the Pacific basin during the next century. Another source of concern is the possible spread of weapons-grade material (enriched uranium and plutonium) and nuclear expertise from the states of the former Soviet Union, including Russia, into the hands of rogue-state or nonstate actors, including terrorists.

The preceding summary of post–Cold War nuclear threats is not exhaustive, and we will have more to say about the problem of proliferation per se. For the moment the issue is the relationship between new threat assessments and the demand curve for NMD. These changes in the international landscape of threat assessment, as well as improved technology for nonnuclear ground-based missile defenses, led the Clinton administration in 1999 to declare that it would make a decision about possible NMD deployment no later than fall 2000. The president then postponed a decision until the next administration. The

Clinton NMD plan, if deployment is approved in 2000, calls for the first deployed systems to appear in 2005. Democrats are being pushed by Republicans toward NMD as well. Presidential candidate George W. Bush announced in 1999 that if elected president in 2000 he would support deployment of U.S. national missile defenses. Republican majorities in Congress sparked passage of several pieces of legislation during Clinton's second term calling for immediate or later deployment of NMD based on available or near-term deployable technology.

Is Russia opposed to nationwide BMD for the same reason that the Soviet leadership was? Undoubtedly Russia fears that U.S. defense technology is well ahead of its own. Some have said that this should not matter to Russia, since the post–Cold War relationship between the United States and Russia is one of "strategic partnership" and not rivalry. Strategic partnership between Washington and Moscow is not to be despised and is to be encouraged on all those issues where it can contribute to mutual security. But strategic partnership cannot obviate geopolitical reality. Russia's geopolitical reality is that is has long, porous, and vulnerable borders, with NATO having incorporated Russia's western security glacis and Russia's underfed, underpaid, and underequipped troops helpless to prevent it. So the nuclear balance between Russia and the United States, in one perverse and unintended way, matters more in the post–Cold War world than it did during the Cold War, at least for Russians.

In theory, the nuclear balance between Russia and the United States should allow for offensive force reductions down to START III levels or even lower, with the cooperation of Britain, France, and China. In theory, the United States and Russia should also be able to find a way to mutually agree on amendments to the ABM Treaty to permit limited NMD, perhaps jointly coordinated by shared early warning and communications. In practice, where military possibilities are corroded by political realities, it is unlikely that the United States and the Russian government can agree on both significant offensive force reductions and BMD deployments based on an amended or abrogated ABM Treaty. Russia sees U.S. missile defenses as part of a future offense–defense mix that could permit a U.S. first strike against Russia's deterrent while nullifying Russia's retaliatory strike. That this scenario is a carry-forward from the Cold War is true, but possibly irrelevant for Russian leaders whose tendency to "worst case" scenarios can only increase along with the financial and other difficulties in rebuilding Russia's military. More realistic is the Russian fear that, although neither the United States nor NATO is likely to attack Russia, nuclear superiority conferred by missile defenses could be used to coerce Russia diplomatically.

Having tutored themselves on the copious supply of studies from U.S. think tanks and other Western sources, Russians are also aware that the current and near-term generations of BMD technology are only the first steps into an unknown military-technology future. Space-based weapons that can attack targets in space or on the earth, perhaps at the speed of light, are the key to future aerospace dominance. Future aerospace dominance by space-based, postnuclear weapons such as lasers or particle beams would bring an end to the nuclear revolution and, in the hands of states other than Russia, advertise Russia's permanent military backwardness. The end of nuclear preeminence is the possible end of Russia as a great power, and that is the possible beginning to the opening of Russia to military subjugation of the kind that it has not experienced in centuries, even if Russia is held together politically in the next century.

NONPROLIFERATION

If ballistic missile defenses are an area of potential Russian conflict with the United States and NATO, what of nuclear nonproliferation? Will Russia follow the Soviet Cold War pattern of collaboration with the United States and international organizations in order to discourage nuclear proliferation? Or will Russia contribute to the spread of nuclear weapons and delivery systems, either directly by exporting them to interested buyers or indirectly by opposing U.S. and other nonproliferation efforts, including international inspection regimes?

Russia's need for hard currency as well as a growing demand for weapons of mass destruction and delivery systems creates a natural community of interest. Russian scientists who can no longer support their families on low wages or wages many months in arrears are also tempted by lucrative offers from foreign countries. On the other hand, Russia wants to maintain its status as the second-ranking nuclear power after the United States, and Russia must also consider the regionalization of nuclear capabilities as a potential source of conflict inimical to Russian interests. The declared nuclear status of India and Pakistan in 1998 brings additional problems of deterrence into an already troubled neighborhood in South Asia. In Northwest Asia, North Korea's on-again, off-again flirtation with nuclear capabilities cannot help but encourage South Korea and Japan into more explicit consideration of their own national nuclear options.

Both the United States and Russia will be faced with the fact of proliferation in the next century, including the spread of nuclear weapons beyond the controlled and contained proliferation of WMD during most of the Cold War. U.S. and Soviet nuclear umbrellas protected states and regions that were thereby sanctuarized against nuclear coercion. Now the Soviet version of extended nuclear deterrence to allies and clients is gone. In addition, nuclear weapons and other WMD no longer are the trumps on the high-technology scale. Twenty-first-century warfare will emphasize nonnuclear precision weapons and their supporting information, communication and electronics systems (sometimes abbreviated as C4I, for command, control, communications, computers, and intelligence). Two impressive demonstrations of the power and precision of U.S. air power bracketed the first decade after the Cold War: the Gulf War of 1991 and Operation Allied Force against Yugoslavia in 1999. Each made clear in a different way that no other state can match American dominance of information-driven warfare for at least several decades into the next century, if then.

Therefore, nuclear weapons become the weapons of choice for dissatisfied regional powers who want to deter U.S. precision strikes and information-based warfare against their military expansion. Unable to match the United States and other high-technology economies in information-based, nonnuclear warfare, aspiring regional hegemons in the Middle East, Southwest Asia, or elsewhere may see in nuclear weapons the leverage of the weaker against the stronger. This possibility of nuclear weapons being used as the main counters to U.S. or NATO force projection couples the questions of deterrence and proliferation on the American policy agenda.

Two schools of thought characterize the U.S. approach to nuclear proliferation. One school, continuous with the dominant tendency in Cold War thinking, holds that any spread of nuclear weapons is inherently bad. All states aspiring to nuclear arsenals should be discouraged, and all states now having acknowledged nuclear forces (with the exception of the five permanent members of the U.N. Security Council, of course) should be urged to roll them back. Another school of thought sees the first approach as doomed to failure in the twenty-first century, regardless of its accomplishments during the Cold War. The second school of thought favors selective U.S. opposition to cases of nuclear or other WMD proliferation, based on the willingness of the state in question to adhere to acceptable norms of international behavior. Of course, the predominant norm in question is nonaggression. According to the second school, the United States and international control regimes would not necessarily attempt to dissuade or to discourage proliferators in states apparently satisfied with the international status quo, or at least in states not so dissatisfied that they were prepared to disrupt the status quo by threats or by war.

Since the status quo works to U.S. advantage in the present and immediate future international system, the selective approach to nonproliferation appears heavily tendentious to those on the receiving end of U.S. disapproval. Why, for example, should India and Pakistan feel the sting of American disapproval for their avowed nuclearism while Israel suffered neither public nor private disapprobation for its "bomb in the basement" nuclear status? In the case of U.S. NATO allies such as Britain and France, it could be argued that the NATO defense pact gives American officials continuing contact with British and

French counterparts and might act in some circumstances as a restraint on an otherwise unilateral decision for nuclear use. But Israel is part of no such alliance and its nuclear decisions are accountable only to its own state interests. Israel, given its perceived defense predicament and small territorial size, makes a strong case for its own nuclear deterrent: to deter any nuclear or other WMD attack against Israel, in order to guarantee against the possibility of another Holocaust, and to deny adversaries the opportunity for nuclear coercion. Despite this logic, Third World and other states aspiring to nuclear status cannot help but notice the selective way in which U.S. nonproliferation norms have been applied. This point, among others, has led some states to withhold their signatures from the Comprehensive Test Ban Treaty, urged by the Clinton administration and opened for signature in 1996.

The selective approach to instances of nuclear proliferation suffers not only from the critique of inconsistency or of hypocrisy. It also invites the state on the cusp of going nuclear to manipulate the United States and its allies in order to obtain economic, political, or other favors for its abstinence: a form of prenuclear blackmail. North Korea has played this game with a highly nuanced diplomacy since 1994, and few have noticed. The United States and its allies, along with the International Atomic Energy Agency, have been made into the experimental mice in the cage designed by North Korea. In return for U.S., Japanese, and South Korean agreement to provide alternatives to nuclear fuel and to fund the construction of reactors for peaceful purposes, North Korea has agreed (for how long?) not to enter the ranks of declared nuclear-weapons states. Publicly released U.S. intelligence estimates of North Korea's nuclear status read like pronouncements from the Oracle at Delphi. For less than unequivocal guarantees that North Korea is not now (for the time being) a nuclear-weapons state, the United States and its allies will ante up to help bail out Pyongyang's dying economy.

North Korea learned something from Saddam Hussein. Having survived the Gulf War in power, he determined to rebuild his weapons of mass destruction, including nuclear, biological, and chemical capabilities. Thus began a decade long *pas de deux* with IAEA inspectors and U.S. policy makers, punctuated by occasional clashes between American enforcers of the no fly zones over Iraq and Iraqi military forces trying to shoot them down. The Clinton administration periodically launched air and missile attacks, primarily against Iraqi military and command targets, most recently during Operation Desert Fox in 1999. However, the aftershock of Desert Fox was that international inspectors for WMD were now removed from Iraq and another round of negotiations would be necessary to get them back into the country. This game of inspect-and-cheat will continue until Saddam Hussein is winkled out of power by domestic forces, an unlikely prospect, or by foreign invasion, even more unlikely. The Iraqi dictator spat in the face of international nonproliferation norms even after losing a war and, as of the last day of the last year of the twentieth century, got away with his bombs and his braggadocio.

This lesson is uncomfortable for the United States because Saddam Hussein represents the most egregious case of an aspiring regional hegemon with clear ambitions to inflict weapons of mass destruction on his immediate neighborhood (or, at the very least, to use them for coercion in lieu of destruction). But more troubling in the long run for U.S. nonproliferation or counterproliferation policy is the potential acquisition by Iran of nuclear weapons. Iran has grievances against a long list of potential victims of an eventual Iranian nuclear coercion or attack: the United States, Israel, Iraq, and Russia, among others. There is no assumption here that Iran would be "careless" with the bomb any more so than India, Pakistan, or Israel might be. But India, Pakistan, and Israel are far less hostile to the international political status quo than Iran, and except for Indian and Pakistani rumbles with one another, devoid of any immediate casus belli. The mutual antagonism between New Delhi and Islamabad is indeed a disturbing case of regional nuclear rivalry and not one that the United States should applaud. But it also not a case that the United States or anyone else could have prevented. India, in particular, is already making known its interest in playing a great-power role in international politics in the twenty-first century, and India's population, resources, and soft power (intellectual capital) make this ambition not unreasonable.

The Clinton administration added a second tier to U.S. nonproliferation policy by its discussion of counterproliferation as a policy option for certain cases. In so doing, it gave an implicit acknowledgment that not all cases of proliferation are the same or deserve similar treatment. Counterproliferation is an attempt to reverse or undo instances of nuclear-weapons spread or of imminent nuclear capabilities not yet realized, either by persuasion or by coercion. In selected instances the coercion might include the use of force: presumably, conventional attacks against nuclear weapons complexes and other infrastructure of an all-but-nuclear state with hostile objectives. Counterproliferation, it can be inferred, might be preemptive or preventive. Preemptive counterproliferation might take place in order to destroy an already existing nuclear capability in the hands of an aggressive state bent on coercion or war against regional neighbors or others. Preventive counterproliferation would take place earlier, in order to preclude the development or deployment of a nuclear-weapons capability on the part of a state whose motives for doing so were judged extremely adverse to U.S. or allied interests.

Counterproliferation in either its preventive or preemptive form is obviously going to be selective, whether nonproliferation policy is officially so. No state can afford to squeeze the pips out of every orange.

The United States faces two difficulties in marshaling support for preventive or preemptive counterproliferation. The first is the need to obtain domestic approval for an act of war, if necessary. The second is the advantage of obtaining allied support in order to share the burdens and risks of war, if necessary, and in order to add legitimacy to the counterproliferation effort. Neither task will be easy as the options move along the continuum from coercive diplomacy to war. Even the threat of war against a nuclear arsenal already in place raises the possibility of collateral damage among the civilian population of the target country, an issue sure to be noticed by American media and by Congress. Counterproliferation short of war may not do the job of disarming or dissuading the hostile power; on the other hand, counterproliferation in the form of actual military attacks raises other legal and public-policy issues that U.S. officials may prefer not to confront. Congress, for example, was unable to fully come to grips with the precedent set by NATO air strikes on Yugoslavia in 1999: It could neither declare war nor invoke the War Powers Act in order to limit the ability of the president to keep U.S. forces in battle without a declaration of war.

Counterproliferation, in other words, must be selective because the means and the will are lacking for ubiquitous intervention and because the price of bringing some recalcitrants to heel might be too high to pay. But because counterproliferation must be selective, it does not follow that the spread of nuclear weapons should be encouraged or treated with resignation. Nothing is automatic in world affairs: A large number of nuclear-armed states might keep a Hobbesian peace.[8] But that outcome is extremely unlikely, given what we know of states' propensities for demonizing their opponents and for playing dangerous cards when the stakes are high. The Cold War provided a test of nuclear stability based on laboratory conditions: two dominant nuclear superpowers, few other nuclear-armed states, system bipolarity, and time for the United States and the Soviet Union to work out rules of the road about how they behaved in arms races and in crises. These laboratory conditions permitted the time and leisure for states to engage in nuclear learning about how to safely and securely operate nuclear forces. The same conditions allowed thorny problems of command and control over nuclear forces to be worked out so that states could reconcile the requirements for negative control (prevention of accidental launch or political usurpation of command) with the capability for positive control (guaranteed response to authorized launch commands).

Absent the same laboratory conditions, nuclear permissiveness in the new world order is ill advised. Admittedly this conclusion seems unfair to nuclear-aspiring states that have no track record of willful aggression against neighbors or against others. But equity is less important in this regard than system management in the interests of peace and security. System management can only be accomplished by the leading states of the system, assisted by international regimes that they themselves must support. It will be harder to contain the spread of nuclear weapons and other WMD in the twenty-first century than it was in the preceding century, but that argues for selective pessimism about nuclear-weapons spread. Selective pessimism means that the United States and other nuclear powers would seek to prevent those cases of proliferation that could be prevented at an acceptable cost, and to work with those cases that cannot be prevented in order to help make those states' arsenals as safe and secure as possible. Selective pessimism would also encourage the United States and other nuclear great powers to continue their efforts toward strategic arms reductions and to improve the quality of their remaining forces so that they are less dependent on hair-trigger responses in order to fulfill war plans.

Where, in a strategy of selective pessimism, does deterrence connect to nonproliferation? Neither the United States nor other states can escape the need to practice deterrence in the new world order, but some of the rules of the game by which deterrence operated between 1946 and 1991 have now changed. Conventional deterrence, not nuclear, is now on the front end of U.S. strategy, and the main threat is perceived to be major regional conflicts, not world war. Deterrence by denial instead of by punishment now rules the strategic roost.

But the credible threat of retaliatory punishment is not excluded from dealing with potential or actual proliferators, including nonstate actors, who behave in antisystemic or anormative ways. The capability for conventional retaliation against the command and control vitals of an enemy state poised for WMD attack, including life-threatening attacks on enemy leadership, can get the attention of even hard cases. Even after the fact of an attack against U.S. forces or values with, say, biological weapons, conventional retaliation can pose some costly options to which few if any perpetrators could respond in kind. Of course, one response to U.S. conventional superiority is to go around or underneath it, with terrorist attacks that are deniable as to their source. But attackers need to fear that American or allied intelligence will eventually cull their correct identities from the fog of information. Once the identities of terrorists or state actors committing WMD attacks have been established, retaliation should be prompt and decisive *pour encourager les autres.*

If new technology makes antinuclear defenses viable in the next century, will that change the relationship between deterrence and proliferation? This depends very much on how good the defense technology is and who owns it. There was a noticeable shift in the U.S. domestic policy debate about missile defense during President Clinton's second term. As of 2000, momentum seems to be on the side of those favoring some kind of national missile defense against limited strikes. Various technologies for airborne or ground-based intercept of ballistic missiles seemed more promising at the end of the 1990s than they did a decade earlier. However, technological innovation does not by itself constitute a strategic breakthrough. Strategy involves a reactive opponent. Offensive countermeasures exist for many of the kinds of defenses that have been proposed. The era of offense-dominant nuclear strategy will probably continue unless and until space-based defenses operating at the speed of light can be deployed and protected. Until then, we are talking not about a shift from offense dominance to defense dominance, as Reagan aspired to, but a more complex and nuanced shift from offense dominance to offense–defense competitiveness.

If antimissile defenses get to the point at which they are more cost effective at the margin than ballistic missile offenses, then the effect will almost certainly be to dissuade interest in ballistic missile strikes, whether armed with nuclear or other weapons. There are other ways to deliver nuclear weapons: One need not rely mainly or exclusively on missiles that lend themselves to interception and destruction. More important, if antimissile defenses become good enough to make missile strikes obsolete, those defenses will have ominous offensive or first-strike capabilities against a variety of target sets and raise the problem of preemption to another technological level. Defenses that can intercept ICBMs or SLBMs may also be able to kill satellites efficiently in order to disrupt communications, command, and control and to deny the opponent a clear picture of the pertinent battlespace. Competent antimissile defenses or other space-based weapons, that is to say, may be the leading edge of a dominant information-warfare strategy for the twenty-first century.

NUCLEAR ABOLITION AND DESENSITIZATION

Since the end of the Cold War a variety of proposals have been put forward to make nuclear arsenals smaller in size well below START III levels, perhaps down to several hundred or fewer warheads for each nuclear possessor, including the United States, Russia, Britain, France, and China among major nuclear powers. In addition to these proposals for vertical disarmament, or structural arms control, others have supported measures for horizontal disarmament, or operational arms control. An exhaustive catalog of these proposals is not possible here.[9] Some of the more interesting or influential proposals for operational arms control aim at what I would prefer to call "nuclear desensitization." Nuclear desensitization makes states less fearful of surprise attack and/or less concerned about falling behind in an arms race. It becomes more important as the numbers of nuclear weapons in the hands of various states comes down (i.e., if structural or vertical disarmament succeeds). Smaller and less diverse arsenals are more vulnerable mutatis mutandis than larger and more diverse ones. However, advocates of nuclear desensitization argue that their proposals have the primary objective of building confidence and transparency between nuclear-armed states, and that these goals are as important for states with larger weapons inventories as for those with smaller holdings. The term "desensitization" is preferred to describe these proposals because sensitivity implies reactive interdependency: Each nuclear state observers and reacts to what others do, especially if there is any likelihood of future conflict with another nuclear power.

The following list summarizes some of the measures for nuclear desensitization that have been proposed by various parties since the end of the Cold War or even during it. Some of these proposed measures for nuclear desensitization also involve manipulating the sizes of force structures or the mix of force components:[10]

Proposed Measure	Implementation	Positive Negatives
Dealerting	No strategic nuclear weapons would be reliant upon prompt launch (launch on warning) for survivability	Verification Measure is easily reversed
Removal of warheads from launchers or deactivation of launchers	Warheads would be stored separately from launch vehicles Launchers might be converted to make rapid reactivation impossible	Crisis might see competitive race to reload warheads on launchers, provoke instability
Virtual arsenals	No ready-made bombs are available, but the capability to do so rapidly, if necessary, remains	Verification Bomb in the basement
SLBMs only	Remove ICBMs and bombers from launcher inventory	Submarines must remain invulnerable to detection Deterrent rests on a single component
Antimissile defenses based on new principles, permitting a defense-protected builddown or even eventual abolition of nuclear weapons	Space-based sensors, ground- or space-based launchers, and kill vehicles, improved BMC3 for missile defense	Antimissile defense technology can be used for offensive purposes (e.g., destroying warning and communication satellites)

The desensitization measures have been listed in order, from the least demanding (dealerting) to the most demanding (missile defenses and supporting battle management and command control). Some of these measures would involve no change in force structure; others would demand considerable reductions in current forces or the elimination of entire classes of launchers.

There is no shortage of proposals, but proposals and good thoughts do not convert themselves into policy agenda items that can be sold to government officials. In the United States there is a tendency for strategy to fall out from the drift of available technology: We justify what technology allows us to do. This was true of the decision to deploy MIRV warheads for ballistic missiles, and it may now be true for the decision to deploy national missile defenses. Sweet technology is more visible and appealing than the seemingly modest objectives of transparency and confidence building. The case for nuclear transparency must be based on political arguments that the avoidance of accidental or inadvertent nuclear war is a shared interest among states, regardless of their other policy proclivities or disagreements.

The dilemma for these and other arms control proposals is that states can readily agree on measures that have comparatively little impact on the existing order of things. Those measures that threaten vested interests within states, including military services and their missions or budgets, will meet obdurate resistance. Arms control works at the margin of states' vital interests most of the time. But the marginal utility of arms control is still important. A future crisis might be assuaged by transparency measures put into effect now. As with deterrence, success in crisis management is often unproved or undetected because the disasters that might have happened were avoided. The same holds for nonproliferation and its relationship to deterrence. In the short term, more-secure deterrence among the existing nuclear powers strengthens a viable nonproliferation regime. Trigger-happy nuclear powers do not provide a good model for emulation.

But in the longer term, aspiring nuclear states will copy what the existing major international powers do, not what they say. If the nuclear Big Five continue to act as if nuclear weapons are the ticket for admission to great-power status, then nonproliferation will be harder. Even further reductions in U.S. and Russian strategic nuclear forces will do little to slake states' appetites for weapons of mass destruction, unless and until Britain, France, and China enter into a multilateral five-power regime to engage in vertical and horizontal nuclear restraint. We are far from that desirable destination. Thus, nuclear deterrence, with all its limitations and vulnerabilities, cannot be put into receivership just yet.

NOTES

1. The U.S. policy debate is in the process of undergoing a tectonic shift on this very issue. According to one authoritative study, "It seems certain that active defenses will play a growing role in U.S. strategy and in the strategy of others in the early decades of the next century." See Center for Counterproliferation Research, National Defense University, and Center for Global Security Research, Lawrence Livermore National Laboratory, *U.S. Nuclear Policy in the 21st Century: A Fresh Look at National Strategy and Requirements* (Washington, D.C.: U.S. Government Printing Office, 1998), 2.43. For counterarguments skeptical of national missile defenses, see John Steinbruner, "National Missile Defense: Collision in Progress," *Arms Control Today* 29, no. 7 (1999): 3–6.

2. For clarity on this topic, I recommend William E. Odom, *The Collapse of the Soviet Military* (New Haven.: Yale University Press, 1998), 1–15, and Raymond L. Garthoff, *Deterrence and the Revolution in Soviet Military Doctrine* (Washington, D.C.: The Brookings Institution, 1990), 6–28.

3. For assessments of the nuclear past and its relationship to the nuclear future, see Colin S. Gray, *The Second Nuclear Age* (Boulder, Colo.: Lynne Rienner, 1999); Stephen J. Cimbala, *The Past and Future of Nuclear Deterrence* (Westport, Conn.: Praeger, 1998); and Keith B. Payne, *Deterrence in the Second Nuclear Age* (Lexington: University Press of Kentucky, 1996).

4. On the sociopolitical level of military doctrine, see Marshal N. V. Ogarkov, *Istoriya uchit bditel'nosti* (History Teaches Vigilance) (Moscow: Voennoe Izdatel'stvo, 1985), 75–76. On the military–technical aspects of military doctrine, see pp. 76–77.

5. Ghulam Dastagir Wardak, comp. and Graham Hall Turbiville, Jr., ed., *The Voroshilov Lectures: Materials from the Soviet General Staff Academy*, vol. 1 (Washington, D.C.: National Defense University Press, 1989), 63–78.

6. Anatoly Klimenko, "The Basis of Russia's Military Doctrine," *Military Parade*, <http://www.ru>, 30 December 1999.

7. Commission to Assess the Ballistic Missile Threat to the United States, *Executive Summary* (Washington, D.C.: U.S. Government Printing Office, 1998).

8. For contrasting arguments on this point, see Scott D. Sagan and Kenneth N. Waltz, *The Spread of Nuclear Weapons: A Debate* (New York: W. W. Norton, 1995), esp. Chapters 1 and 2.

9. See Jonathan Schell, "The Gift of Time: The Case for Abolishing Nuclear Weapons," *The Nation*, 2–9 February 1998, for interviews with former policy makers, academics, and other nuclear experts favoring broader measures for strutural or operational (vertical or horizontal) nuclear disarmament.

10. My discussions with Bruce Blair, Keith Payne, and Leon Sloss over many years have contributed to my thoughts in this section. They are not responsible for this list nor for the arguments behind it.

Suggestions for Further Reading

Best, Melvin L., Jr., John Hughes-Wilson, and Andrei A. Piontkowsky. *Strategic Stability in the Post–Cold War World and the Future of Nuclear Disarmament*. Dordrecht: Kluwer Academic Publishers, 1995.

Blair, Bruce G. *The Logic of Accidental Nuclear War*. Washington, D.C.: The Brookings Institution, 1993.

Brodie, Bernard. *Strategy in the Missile Age*. Princeton, N.J.: Princeton University Press, 1959.

Bundy, McGeorge. *Danger and Survival*. New York: Random House, 1985.

Center for Counterproliferation Research, National Defense University, and Center for Global Security Research, Lawrence Livermore National Laboratory. *U.S. Nuclear Policy in the 21st Century: A Fresh Look at National Strategy and Requirements*. Washington, D.C.: U.S. Government Printing Office, 1998.

Cimbala, Stephen J. *The Past and Future of Nuclear Deterrence*. Westport, Conn.: Praeger, 1998.

Dunn, Lewis A. *Controlling the Bomb*. New Haven: Yale University Press, 1982.

Flourney, Michele, ed. *Nuclear Weapons After the Cold War*. New York: Harper Collins, 1993.

George, Alexander L., and Richard Smoke. *Deterrence in American Foreign Policy: Theory and Practice*. New York: Columbia University Press, 1974.

Gray, Colin S. *The Second Nuclear Age*. Boulder, Colo.: Lynne Rienner, 1999.

Jervis, Robert. *The Meaning of the Nuclear Revolution*. Ithaca, N.Y.: Cornell University Press, 1989.

Kent, Glenn A., and David E. Thaler. *First-Strike Stability and Strategic Defenses: Part II of a Methodology for Evaluating Strategic Forces, R-3918-AF*. Santa Monica, Calif.: RAND Corporation, 1990.

Mueller, John E. *Retreat from Doomsday: The Obsolescence of Major War*. New York: Basic Books, 1989.

Payne, Keith B. *Deterrence in the Second Nuclear Age*. Lexington: University Press of Kentucky, 1996.

Pry, Peter V. *War Scare: Russia and America on the Nuclear Brink*. Westport, Conn.: Praeger, 1999.

Quester, George H. *Deterrence Before Hiroshima: The Airpower Background of Modern Strategy*. 2d ed. New Brunswick, N.J.: Transaction Books, 1986.

Schelling, Thomas C. *Arms and Influence*. New Haven: Yale University Press, 1966.

Spector, Leonard. *Nuclear Ambitions*. Boulder, Colo.: Westview Press, 1990.

Index

Accidental, inadvertent, and/or unauthorized launches (war), 43, 49, 58, 76, 120, 133, 158, 163, 173

American (U.S.) nuclear umbrella (extended nuclear deterrence), 1, 12, 15, 17–18, 54, 108, 165

Antiballistic missile (ABM) defenses, 4, 57, 73, 75–79, 97, 173

Anti-Ballistic Missile (ABM) Treaty, 25, 26, 39, 51, 81, 97, 123, 132, 134, 161, 163, 164

Arms reductions (United States and Russia), 4, 17, 67–69, 122–123, 124; antiballistic missile (ABM) defenses, 73; Bayesian methods, 73, 85, 99; breaking out of treaty agreements, 92–95; first-strike stability, 68, 70, 72–73, 74, 75, 76, 79–80, 82; nuclear abolition and desensitization, 171–174; START treaties, 67–68, 69–71, 81, 82, 83, 93, 96, 98; strategic nuclear forces, 69–71; summary and observations, 95–100; valued assets, 72

Arms reductions (United States and Russia) and future deterrence, 74–75; effect of ABM defenses, 75–79; effect of lower alert rates, 79–80; geopolitical stability and alert rates, 80–83

Arms reductions (United States and Russia) launch on warning, 69, 72, 74, 84; feasibility of, 85; motivation for, 84–85; warning-system messages and confidence levels, 85–92

Asia, 27, 30, 32, 34, 107, 113, 132, 165, 166

Aum Shinrikyo, 35

Ballistic missile defenses (BMD), 4, 49–52, 122, 123, 132, 134, 164, 165. *See also* Antiballistic missile (ABM) defenses

Bell, Robert, 92

Biological weapons. *See* Chemical, biological, or nuclear weapons

Blair, Bruce, 175 n.10

Bomber force(s), 6, 8, 14, 16, 71, 72, 82, 84, 95, 97, 173; U.S. strategic-retaliatory forces, 121, 122, 124, 125, 127, 130, 136

Brezhnev, Leonid (regime), 157

About the Editor and Contributors

Stephen J. Cimbala is a professor of political science at Penn State University (Delaware County). He has contributed to the literature of national security studies, defense, arms control, and military strategy for more than twenty years. Among his recent publications are *Coercive Military Strategy* (1998) and *The Past and Future of Nuclear Deterrence* (1998). Dr. Cimbala is a past recipient of the university's Eisenhower Award for distinguished teaching. He serves on the editorial board of five professional journals and has taken part in a variety of military exercises, simulations, and other practica in the Department of Defense and in the military services. He is a consulting expert to the U.S. Department of State on arms control.

Lewis A. Dunn is a corporate vice president of Science Applications International Corporation (SAIC) and director of SAIC's Center for Counterproliferation Analysis. Dr. Dunn's recent work has focused on protecting population from CBW attack, strengthening U.S. CBW deterrence and defense capabilities, proliferation warning and surprise, and future directions for nuclear arms control options. He is a former assistant director of the U.S. Arms Control and Disarmament Agency and served as ambassador to the 1985 Nuclear Nonproliferation Treaty Review Conference. Dr. Dunn is the author of *Controlling the Bomb* (1982) and *Containing Nuclear Proliferation*, Adelphi Paper No. 263 (1992). He has authored numerous papers, reports, and articles on nonproliferation and counterproliferation, national security, and arms control policy and compliance issues.

William C. Martel is a professor of national security affairs at the Naval War College. Dr. Martel has been a postdoctoral research fellow and MacArthur scholar at Harvard University's Center for Science and International Affairs in the Kennedy School of Government, and at the Center for International Affairs. While at Harvard he conducted research on nuclear proliferation and democratic reform in Russia, and was a member of the project team that wrote the book *Cooperative Denuclearization: From Pledges to Deeds* (1993). He was a member of the professional staff of the RAND Corporation in Washington, D.C. He is the author of numerous articles and books, and has written for the *Wall Street Journal* and *Christian Science Monitor*. He was associate professor of international relations and Russian studies and founder and director of the Center for Strategy and Technology at the Air War College. He is involved with the USAF Scientific Advisory Board, directs various studies on defense technology and policy matters for the Defense Advanced Research Projects Agency (DARPA), serves as the editor of the occasional papers series at the Center for Strategy and Technology, and is a member of the International Institute of Strategic Studies.

Frederic S. Nyland is a consultant with the U.S. Department of State. He is a specialist in operational research and systems analysis as they apply to the reduction of nuclear weapons, strategic stability, proliferation of weapons of mass destruction, and ballistic missile defense issues. Prior to joining the U.S. Arms Control and Disarmament Agency and the state department, Nyland wrote many reports on military affairs at Lockheed Martin, and the RAND Corporation, where he was the director of national security research (Washington office). He has contributed to a number of books, including *Espana, Que Defensa?* (1981); *Strategic Nuclear Targeting* (1986); and *Strategic Stability in the Post–Cold War World and the Future of Nuclear Disarmament* (1995). His professional affiliations include the Arms Control Association, the Military Operations Research Society, and the Denver World Affairs Council.

George H. Quester is a professor of government and politics at the University of Maryland, where he teaches courses on international relations, U.S. Foreign policy, and international military security. Dr. Quester has also taught at Cornell and Harvard Universities, at UCLA, and in the department of military strategy at the National War College. From 1991 to 1993 he served as Olin Visiting Professor at the U.S. Naval Academy. He is the author of a number of books and articles on international security issues and broader questions of international relations, and is a member of the International Institute for Strategic Studies and the Council on Foreign Relations.

James Scouras is a principal scientist at DynMeridian's Arms Control Technology Center, providing technical and analytical support to the Defense Threat Reduction Agency's Office of Science and Technology. His research emphasizes the development and application of innovative quantitative analytical techniques to fundamental issues in international security, arms control, ballistic missile defenses, and proliferation of nuclear weapons. He is also an independent consultant to the State Department and an adjunct employee of the Institute for Defense Analyses. Previously, he was a physicist at the RAND Corporation and Associate Director of the Strategic Weapon Systems Department at System Planning Corporation.